Kindred Moon Paranormal Survival Guide to Spiritual Warfare and Protection

Copyright © 2017 Michael D. McDonald

All rights reserved.

ISBN: 9781795425216

DEDICATION

Above all else, this is for my daughter, Brittney Storm.

INTRODUCTION

Throughout history, holy wars have taken many souls.

In the ongoing battle between good and evil the balance continually shifts. These battles have been fought by gods, angels, devils, and human beings. For example; Jesus stands for all that is good while Satan stands for evil. Hercules for good and Chthonic Monsters for evil.

Even Hollywood appoints the "good vs evil" concept such as in the classic westerns where the good guys rode on white horses while villains rode a black steed. Star Wars used "light side of the force" as a representation of the noble Jedi while the "dark side of the force" was reserved for the insidious Sith.

Many people have lost their lives in these holy wars, from the Knights Templar and the Knights of the Crusades all the way up to present day orders. This includes terrorists who murder innocents in the name of their spiritual beliefs.

Heart of Darkness, by Joseph Conrad, perfectly depicts mankind's eternal struggle with their own morals and the battle against the evil dwelling within. Simply put, good is something that will not cause harm while evil is something that will.

I, and the members of Kindred Moon Paranormal, are mostly Christians. However, we do have members of the team that are Wiccan, spiritual, or other religions/beliefs as we do not discriminate. We utilize different views from Christianity to help bring perspective and knowledge to the paranormal investigations and cases. Each view is appreciated if the belief helps protect and doesn't harm anyone or anything involved.

Each religion has a conflicting side along the spectrum. All good has its evil. All white has its black. While I am ordained in the Christian faith, my experience has shown that using different forms of protections and cleansing methods together has been more effective than just one by itself. As an investigator with over 25 years of experience, it is my top priority to keep my team and client's safe through knowledge and faith.

The danger is not exclusive to ghost hunters and paranormal investigators. Everyone is susceptible to the temptations from evil, or the devil himself, including the risk of possession. This book is a survival guide to live a positive spiritual life.

Contents

DEDICATION 3
INTRODUCTION 5
ACKNOWLEDGMENTS 8
CHAPTER 1: HIGHER POWER, RELIGIONS, AND PRACTICES 10
CHAPTER 2: PROTECTION: ITEMS AND METHODS 14
CHAPTER 3: THE EVOLUTION OF GHOST HUNTING EQUIPMENT
.... 62
CHAPTER 4: PARANORMAL THEORIES AND BELIEFS 73
CHAPTER 5: THE FOUR TYPES OF HAUNTINGS 92
CHAPTER 6: DEMONOLOGY-KNOW YOUR ENEMY 105
CHAPTER 7: EXORCISM-EXPEL ALL EVIL AWAY FROM YOU 121
CHAPTER 8: ANGELOLOGY-GUARDIANS & PROTECTORS 149
CHAPTER 9: HOW TO COLLECT PARANORMAL EVIDENCE 197
CHAPTER 10: THE INVESTIGATION 210
CHAPTER 11: REVIEW YOUR EVIDENCE AND FINDINGS 224
CHAPTER 12: CONCLUSION, OFFER BLESSING, & CLEANSING . 233
ADDENDUM: SHADOW BEINGS 236
SUMMATION AND THANKS 242
SPECIAL THANKS 244
LINKS AND RESOURCES 245
ABOUT THE AUTHOR 246
NOTES 247

ACKNOWLEDGMENTS

A lot of Blood sweat and tears went into the making of this book, including many years of cultivating my knowledge and experiences so I can share it with you to prepare you for the world of the paranormal. It took years to complete this book and it was a struggle to get it done in the way it needed to be. I hope you can learn from what I have shared.

Enjoy!

CHAPTER 1: HIGHER POWER, RELIGIONS, AND PRACTICES

There are multitudes of different religions and each have their own belief systems. In this book, I chose to cover three: Christianity, Wicca, and Spirituality related to Native Americans.

Christianity is described as religion based on the word of Jesus Christ through the Bible's sacred scriptures. They believe that Jesus is the Messiah and was sent by God. They also believe that by his dying and rising from the dead, Jesus made up for the sins of Adam and allowed him to enter heaven. They believe that there is one God that exists in three forms; the Father, the Son (Jesus), and the Holy Spirit. They believe that the only way to be cleansed of your sins is to repent and to have faith in the precious blood of Jesus Christ. Baptism shows your authentic in your repentance.

There are three major branches of Christianity which are: Roman Catholicism, Eastern Orthodoxy and Protestantism. However, there are many other subcategories that are within these branches. Christianity has existed since the 1st century and began as a sect of Judaism.

Wiccan Religion, also known as "Wicca", is considered a modern pagan, "witchcraft" religion. This religion was created around the first half of the 20th century and became public in 1954 due to the efforts of Gerald Gardner, considered the "Father of Modern Wicca" (1884-1964). A common theme with Wicca is that Wicca has no higher power, no individual leader, no prophet, and no bible to dictate its laws and beliefs. They believe in the equality of both sexes which makes Wicca a duo theistic religion as they commonly worship gods and goddesses, (traditionally the Moon Goddess and the Horned God). The Wiccan Rede is "If it causes no harm, do what you will".

Wicca as a religion is commonly misunderstood. American culture tends to believe that Wiccans are witches who practice black magic and worship Satan and his disciples. For this reason, I have included their 13 principles of belief.

- Perform rites to regulate ourselves with the natural rhythm of life forces marked by the phases of the moon and the seasonal Quarters and Cross Quarters.
- Seek to live in harmony with nature and ecological balance.
- Accept a depth of power far greater than ordinary, sometimes referred to as "Supernatural" but believe that everyone has the natural potential.
- Perceive the Creative Power in the universe manifests as masculine and feminine and understand that neither one is valued more.
- Recognize both outer and inner (psychological) worlds known as the spiritual world and understand the interaction for the two dimensions is the basis for paranormal phenomena and we honor both as is necessary for fulfillment.
- Do not recognize any authoritarian hierarchy, but do honor those who teach, respect those who share greater knowledge and wisdom, and acknowledge those who give themselves in leadership.
- A worldview and philosophy of life which we identify as Witchcraft whereas religion, magic, and wisdom in living is united in the way one views and lives in the world.
- Witches seek to control the forces within him/herself that make life possible to live wisely and without harm to others and nature.

- Believe in the affirmation and fulfillment of life in a continuation of evolution and development of consciousness giving meaning to the Universe and the role we play in it.
- The only animosity we have against other religions or philosophy of life is their claim that their way is the only way" and has historically denied freedom to others and suppressed differing religious practices and beliefs.
- As American witches, we are concerned with the present and future. We are not threatened by debates of the history of Wicca, origins of various terms, and legitimacy of the differing traditions.
- Do not accept the concept of absolute evil, nor do we worship any entity known as "Satan" or "the Devil". We do not seek power through the suffering of others nor do we accept that personal benefit can be gained only by denial to others.
- Finally, seek within Nature that which contributes to our health and well-being.

The focus of spirituality as related to Native Americans tends to focus on Nature - landscape, animals, plants, and environmental elements. Religion was not a native concept. In fact, mention of religion invoked anxiety with most tribes. The English who invaded their land used religion as a reason to discriminate and was often the cause of great strife to Native Americans. There are many different principles due to the variety of tribes, clans, and other groups and their respective beliefs. Their spiritual principles were difficult for Christians to understand, especially since there was no written book of guidelines. These religious practices include ceremonies and traditions that have been verbally passed down through many generations. Ceremonies often include bountiful feasts, music, traditional dance, and various performances.

Hallucinogens, tobacco, and sweat lodges are examples of things utilized by Native Americans believed to allow greater power to communicate with the gods. Animals are revered within their spirituality and are also used as symbolism representing ideas, characteristics, and spirits. The concept of animal guides and spirit guides will be discussed later in the book.

Native Americans believe strongly in the existence of spirits, both "good" and "evil". Destructive spirits were feared but their existence was vital for the balance of all things. Without negative, there is no positive.

This is a quick overview of a few religions and beliefs. There is such a variety of differing organized religions often with numerous beliefs. I personally do not feel that any specific faith or belief is right or wrong. It is more about what speaks to you and which belief system best fits in with your personal identity.

CHAPTER 2: PROTECTION: ITEMS AND METHODS

This chapter is a quick-reference guide of the different objects and methods used by KMPS when dealing with the paranormal (particularly demons).

Due to the differing views on religions/beliefs, the objects and methods of protection vary.

Protection comes in many forms such as prayers and scripture, crystals and gemstones, candles, herbs and incense, animal and spirit guides, along with other elements. We have used these things at one time or another and they seem to have a greater effect when used in combination.

Our team strongly believes that the more positive energy created by those involved the better, but make the decision as a team. Everyone should agree. No weak links. It is important to be unified and show no vulnerability. These objects and methods are used not only to protect ourselves and our loved ones but also as protection for the tormented people who are the target of the demonic/negative entity.

BINDING & REBUKING (COMMANDING EVIL SPIRITS)

Binding an evil spirit is using the authority of Jesus Christ and his power to make the evil spirit stop whatever it is doing and not make any further progress. To rebuke is to issue a very direct order by a person with direct authority with the expectation of instant, compete, and final obedience of the order. To take authority over the evil spirit, stop its intentions, and send it back to the pits of Hell.

CHRISTIAN PRAYERS & SCRIPTURE

The Lord's Prayer
Our Father who art in heaven, hallowed by thy name, thy kingdom come, thy will be done on earth as it is in heaven. Give us this day our daily bread and forgive us our trespasses as we forgive those who trespass against us and lead us not into temptation but deliver us from evil. Amen.

Angel of God
Angel of God, my guardian dear, to whom God's love commits me here. Ever this day (or night) be at my side; to light, to guard, to rule, and guide. Amen.

Hail Mary
Hail Mary, full of grace, the lord is with thee. Blessed is the fruit of thy womb, Jesus. Holy Mary, Mother of God, pray for us sinners, now and at the hour of our death. Amen.

Prayer to Love God
God, my father, may I love you in all things and above all things. May I reach the joy which you have prepared for me in heaven. Nothing is good that is against your will, and all that is good comes from your hand. Place in my heart a desire to please you and fill my mind with thoughts of your love, so that I may grow in your wisdom and enjoy your peace. Amen.

Under Your Protection
We fly to thy protection, O holy mother of God. Despise not our petitions in our necessities, but deliver us always from dangers O glorious and blessed virgin. Amen.

Prayer to all Angels
All you holy angels and archangels, thrones and dominations, principalities and powers, the virtues of heaven, cherubim and seraphim, praise the lord forever. Amen.

Archangel St. Gabriel
O Captain and leader of the armies of heaven, unworthy as we are, we beseech you without cease to surround us with your intercession and cover us beneath the shelter of the glory of your ethereal wings. We bend our knees and cry out with perseverance: deliver us from danger, O prince of the powers on high! Amen.

Archangel Uriel
Oh holy St. Uriel, come to our aid with your legion of angels! Intercede for us that our hearts may burn with the fire of God. Obtain for us the grace to use the sword of truth to fight against all that is not in conformity to the most adorable will of god in our lives. Amen.

Archangel St. Michael
St. Michael, the archangel, defend us in battle. Be our defense against the wickedness and snares of the devil. May god rebuke him, we humbly pray. And do thou, O prince of the heavenly host, by the power of god, thrust into hell Satan and the other evil spirits who prowl about the world for the ruin of souls. Amen.

Against Every Evil
Spirit of our god, father, son, and holy spirit, most holy trinity, immaculate virgin Mary, angels, archangels, and saints of heaven, descend upon me. Please purify me, lord, mold me, fill me with yourself, use me. Banish all the forces of evil from me, destroy them, vanquish them, so that I can be healthy and do good deeds. Banish from me

all spells, witchcraft, black magic, malefic, ties, maledictions, and the evil eye; diabolic infestations, oppressions, possessions; all that is evil and sinful, jealousy, perfidy, envy; physical, psychological, moral, spiritual, diabolical ailments. Burn all these evils in hell, that they may never again touch me or any other creature in the entire world. I command and bid all the powers who molest me—by the power of god all powerful, in the name of Jesus Christ our savior, through the intercession of the immaculate virgin Mary—to leave me forever, and to be consigned into the everlasting hell, where they will be bound by saint Gabriel, saint Raphael, our guardian angels, and where they will be crushed under the heel of the Immaculate virgin Mary. Amen.

Come Holy Spirit
Come Holy Spirit, fill the hearts of your faithful and kindle in them the fire of your love. Send forth your spirit and they shall be created. And you shall renew the face of the earth. O, God, who by the light of the Holy Spirit we may be truly wise and ever enjoy his consolations, through Christ Our Lord. Amen.

Sign of the Cross
In nomine patris, et filii, et spiritus sancti. Amen
In the name of the father and of the son and the holy spirit. Amen.

Gloria Patri
Glory be to the father and to the son, and to the holy Spirit. As it was in the beginning is now and will be forever. Amen

Anima Christi

Soul of Christ, sanctify me; body of Christ, save me; blood of Christ, inebriate me; water from the side of Christ, wash me; passion of Christ, strengthen me; o good Jesus, hear me; within your wounds, hide me; let me never be separated from you; from the evil one, protect me; at the hour of my death, call me; and bid me to come to you; that with your saints, I may praise you forever and ever Amen.

Breaking Curses

In the name of the Lord Jesus Christ of
Nazareth, by the power of his cross, his blood and his resurrection, I take authority over all curses, hexes, spells, voodoo practices, witchcraft
assignments, satanic rituals, incantations and evil wishes that have been sent my way, or have passed down the generational bloodline. I break
their influence over my life by the power of the risen Lord Jesus Christ, and I command these curses to go back to where they came from and be replaced with a blessing. I ask for forgiveness for and denounce all
negative inner vows and agreements that I have made with the enemy, and I ask that you Lord Jesus Christ release me from any bondage they may have held me in. I claim your shed blood over all aspects of my life, relationships, ministry endeavors and finances. I thank you for your enduring love, your angelic protection, and for the fullness of your
abundant blessings. Amen.

Prayer Against Evil

Spirit of our god, father, son and holy spirit, most holy trinity, descend upon me. Please purify me, mold me, fill me with yourself, and use me. Banish all the forces of evil from me; destroy them, vanquish them so that I can be healthy and do good deeds. Banish from me all spells, witchcraft, black magic, demonic assignments, malefic, maledictions and the evil eye; diabolic infestations, oppressions, possessions; all that is evil and sinful; jealousy, treachery, envy; all physical, psychological, moral, spiritual and diabolical ailments; as well as all enticing spirits, deaf, dumb, blind, mute and sleeping spirits, new-age spirits, occult spirits, religious spirits, antichrist spirits, and any other spirits of death and darkness. I command and bid all the powers who molest me-by the power of god almighty, in the name of Jesus Christ our savior-to leave me forever, and to be consigned into the everlasting lake of fire, that they may never again touch me or any other creature in the entire world. Amen.

Denouncing the Occult

Heavenly Father, in the name of your only begotten Son, Jesus Christ, I denounce Satan and all his works, all forms of witchcraft, the use of divination, the practice of sorcery, dealing with mediums, channeling with spirit guides, the Ouija board, astrology, Reiki, hypnosis, automatic writing, horoscopes, numerology, all types of fortune telling, palm readings, levitation, and anything else associated with the occult or Satan. I denounce all of them in the name of Jesus Christ who came in the flesh, and by the power of his cross, his blood and his resurrection, I break their hold over my life. I confess these sins before you and ask you to cleanse and forgive me. I ask you Lord Jesus to enter my heart and create in me the kind of person you have intended me to be. I ask you to send forth the gifts of your holy spirit to baptize me, just as you baptized your disciples on the day of Pentecost. I thank you, heavenly father, for strengthening my inner spirit with the power of your holy spirit, so that Christ may dwell in my heart. Through faith, rooted and grounded in love, may I be able to comprehend with all the saints, the breadth, length, height and depth of Christ's love which surpasses all knowledge. Amen.

Breaking Generational Bondage
Dear Lord Jesus Christ, I thank you for your sacrifice on the cross of Calvary for the forgiveness of my sins. Please enforce the power of your cross on all my generational inherited weaknesses, character defects, personality traits, cellular disorders, genetic disorders and tendencies toward sin. Please break all unhealthy soul-ties and forms of enmeshment between me and my parents, grandparents, siblings, offspring, mates and any other unhealthy relationship that my mates had with others in the past. By the power of your command Lord Jesus Christ, I take the sword of the spirit and cut myself free from all generational inherited cellular or genetic disorders, character defects and tendencies toward sin. I sever all unhealthy soul-ties and forms of enmeshment, and in the name of Jesus Christ, I say that I am now free-free to be the child of God the Lord intended me to be. Amen.

Prayer Against Malefice
God, our Lord, King of ages, all powerful and Almighty, you made everything and who transform everything simply by your will; you who changed into dew the flames of the seven-times hotter furnace and protected and saved your three holy children: You are the doctor and physician of my soul. You are the salvation of those who turn to you. I beseech you to make powerless, banish, and drive out every diabolic power, presence and machination; every evil influence, malefice or evil eye and all evil actions aimed against me. Where there is envy and malice, give me an abundance of goodness, endurance, victory and charity. O Lord, you who love man, I beg you to reach out your powerful hands and your most high and mighty arms and come to my aid. Send your angel of peace over me, to protect my body and soul. May he keep at bay and

vanquish every evil power, every poison or malice invoked against me by corrupt and envious people. Then under the protection of your authority may I sing with gratitude, "The Lord is my salvation; whom should I fear?" I will not fear evil because you are with me, my God, my strength, my powerful Lord, Lord of peace, Father of all ages. Amen.

Prayer for a Spiritual Canopy

Dear Lord Jesus, please forgive me for all the times I have not submitted to your will in my life. Please forgive me for all my sinful actions, making agreements with the enemy, and for believing the devil's lies. I now submit to you as my Lord, dear Jesus. Now I break every agreement that I have made with the enemy. Lord Jesus, please have your warring angels remove and bind to the abyss all demons and their devices that had access to me because I believed their lies. I now ask you to establish a hedge of protection around me, over me and under me, and seal it with your blood, Lord Jesus Christ. I now choose to put on the full armor of God and ask that you cleanse me and seal me, body, mind, soul and spirit, with your blood, Lord Jesus Christ. Please have your warring angels bind up and remove all demons, their devices, and all their power from within this protective hedge and have them sent to the abyss. Please have your warriors destroy all demonic, occult or witchcraft assignments directed against me including all backups and replacements. Please have your warriors remove all trafficking people and send them back to their own bodies and seal them there with your blood, Lord Jesus Christ. Please have your angels stand guard over me and protect me from all the attacks of the enemy. Amen.

Prayer to Remove Trafficking People

Dear Lord Jesus, will you please send a special assignment of warring angels to remove all spiritually trespassing people from me. In the name, power and authority of the Lord Jesus Christ of Nazareth who came in the flesh, I cancel all astral assignments over my life. I take dominion over all astral assignments of witchcraft sent against me, and I break their hold right now through the power of the Lord Jesus Christ. Dear Lord Jesus, please have your warring angels strip these witches of their psychic powers, demonic powers and occult powers. Please strip them of psychic visions, powers of divination, and any other craft that allows them to interfere with me. Please have all their powers and devices destroyed and cast into the abyss. I ask you to bring these people before your throne and bless them with a revelation of who you are and your love and plans of salvation for them. Please show them how they are being deceived by Satan. Please have your warriors send them back to their own bodies and seal them there with your blood, Lord Jesus. I thank you for establishing an impenetrable shield of protection all around me; in Jesus' name. Amen.

Binding Evil Spirits

In the name of the Lord Jesus Christ of Nazareth, I stand with the power of the Lord God Almighty to bind Satan and all his evil spirits, demonic forces, satanic powers, principalities, along with all kings and princes of terrors, from the air, water, fire, ground, netherworld, and the evil forces of nature. I take authority over all demonic assignments and functions of destruction sent against me, and I expose all demonic forces as weakened, defeated enemies of Jesus Christ. I stand with the power of the Lord God Almighty to bind all enemies of Christ present together, all demonic entities under their one and highest authority, and I command these spirits into the abyss to never again return. Their assignments and influences are over. I arise today with the power of the Lord God Almighty to call forth the heavenly host, the holy angels of God, to surround and protect, and cleanse with God's holy light all areas vacated by the forces of evil. I ask the Holy Spirit to permeate my mind, heart, body, soul and spirit, creating a hunger and thirst for God's holy word, and to fill me with the life and love of my Lord, Jesus Christ. Amen.

Destroying Demonic Influence
Through the power of Lord Jesus Christ of Nazareth, I come against every source of sin in my life. I ask you Lord Jesus to send forth an assignment of warring angels to strike down and destroy every demonic entity that has been influencing my sinful behaviors of envy, criticism, impatience, resentment, pride, rebellion, stubbornness, unforgiveness, gossip, disobedience, strife, violence, divorce, accusation, anger manipulation, jealousy, greed, laziness, revenge, coveting, possessiveness, control, retaliation, selfishness, deceitfulness, deception, dishonesty, unbelief, seduction, lust, pornography, masturbation, idolatry and witchcraft. May your warring angels strike down and destroy every demonic influence that has contributed to my physical and psychological infirmities of nerve disorder, lung disorder, brain disorder or dysfunction, AIDS, cancer hypochondria, hyperactivity, depression, schizophrenia, fatigue, anorexia, bulimia, addictions, gluttony, perfectionism, alcoholism, self-abuse, sexual addictions, sexual perversions, attempted suicide, incest, pedophilia, lesbianism, homosexuality, adultery homophobia, confusion, ignorance, procrastination, self-hatred, isolation, loneliness, ostracism, paranoia, nervousness, passivity, indecision, doubt, oppression, rejection, poor self-image, anxiety, shame, timidity and fear. I arise today through the power of the Lord Jesus Christ and ask to be filled with the Holy Spirits gifts of

peace, patience, love, joy, kindness, generosity, faithfulness, gentleness, self-control, humility, forgiveness, goodness, fortitude, discipline, truth, relinquishment, good self-image, prosperity, charity, obedience, a sound mind, order, fulfillment in Christ, acceptance of self, acceptance of others, trust, freedom from addictions, freedom of having-to-control, freedom from shame, wholeness, wellness, health, wisdom, knowledge, understanding, and the light and life of the Lord Jesus Christ. Amen.

Prayer for Inner Healing
Dear Lord Jesus, please come and heal my wounded and troubled heart. I beg you to heal the torments that are causing anxiety in my life. I beg you, heal the underlying source of my sinfulness. I beg you to come into my life and heal the psychological harms that struck me in my childhood and from the injuries they have caused throughout my life. Lord Jesus, you know my burdens. I lay them on your good shepherd's heart. I beseech you-by the merits of the great open wound in your heart to heal the small wounds that are in mine. Heal my memories, so that nothing that has happened to me will cause me to remain in pain and anguish, filled with anxiety. Heal, O Lord, all those wounds that have been the cause of evil that is rooted in my life. I want to forgive all those who have offended me. Look to those inner sores that make me unable to forgive. You who came to forgive the afflicted of heart, please, heal my wounded and troubled heart. Heal, O Lord Jesus, all those intimate wounds that are the root cause of my physical illness. I offer you my heart. Accept it, Lord, purify it and give me the sentiments of your divine heart. Heal me, O Lord, from the pain caused by the death of my loved ones. Grant me to regain peace and joy in the knowledge that you are the resurrection and the life. Make me an authentic witness to your resurrection, your victory

over sin and death, and your loving presence among all men. Amen.

Healing the Family Tree
Heavenly Father, I come before you as your child, in great need of your help; I have physical health needs, emotional needs, spiritual needs and interpersonal needs. Many of my problems have been caused by my own failures, neglect and sinfulness, for which I humbly beg your forgiveness, Lord. I also ask you to forgive the sins of my ancestors whose failures have left their effects on me in the form of unwanted tendencies, behavior patterns, and defects in body, mind and spirit. Heal me, Lord, of all these disorders. With your help I sincerely forgive everyone, living and dead members of my family tree, who have directly offended me or my loved ones in any way, or those whose sins have resulted in our present sufferings and disorders. In the name of your divine son Jesus, and in the power of his Holy Spirit, I ask you father, to deliver me and my entire family tree from the influence of the evil one. Free all living and dead members of my family tree, including those in adoptive relationships, and those in extended family relationships, and those in extended family relationships, from every contaminating form of bondage. By your loving concern for us, heavenly father, and by the shed blood of your precious son Jesus, I beg you to extend your blessings to me and all my living and deceased relatives. Heal every negative effect transmitted through all past generations, and prevent such negative effects in future generations of my family tree. I symbolically place the cross of Jesus over the head of each person in my family tree, and between each generation; I ask you to let the cleansing blood of Jesus purify the bloodlines in my family lineage. Send protective angels to encamp around us and administer your divine healing power to all of us, even in areas of genetic disability. Give special power to our family

members' guardian angels to heal, protect, guide and encourage each of us in all our needs. Let your healing power be released at this very moment, and let it continue if your sovereignty permits. In our family, Lord, replace all bondage with a holy bonding of family love. Let there be an ever-deeper bonding with you, Lord, by the Holy Spirit, to your son Jesus. Let the family of the holy trinity pervade our family with its tender, warm, loving presence, so that our family may recognize and manifest that love in all our relationships. All our unknown needs we include with this petition that we pray in Jesus' precious name. Amen.

Denouncing Lodges and Secret Societies
Lord Jesus, I come to you as a sinner seeking forgiveness and healing from all sins committed against you by my family lineage. I honor my earthly father, mother and ancestors, but I utterly turn away from and denounce all their sins, especially those that have exposed me to any kind of harmful influence. I forgive all my ancestors for the effects of their sins and ask to be washed clean of their destructive consequences. I denounce and rebuke Satan and every evil power that has affected my family lineage. I denounce and forsake my involvement in all lodges, secret societies and any other evil craft practiced by my ancestors. I denounce all oaths and rituals in every level and degree. I denounce witchcraft, the spirit of the antichrist and the curse of any demonic doctrine. I denounce idolatry, blasphemy and all destructive forms of secrecy and deception. I denounce the love of power, the love of money, and any fears that have held me in bondage. I denounce all spiritually binding oaths taken in Freemasonry, Mormonism, the Order of Amaranth, Oddfellows, Buffalos, Druids and Foresters Lodges, the Ku Klux Klan, the Grange, the Woodmen of the World, Riders of the Red Robe, the Knights of Pythias, the Mystic Order of the Veiled Prophets of the Enchanted Realm, the

women's Orders of the Eastern Star and of the White Shrine of Jerusalem, the Daughters of the Eastern Star, the International Orders of Job's Daughters, the Rainbow Girls and the boys' Order of DeMolay and any other secret society along with their destructive effects on me and my family. I denounce the blindfold and hoodwink, and any effects they had on my emotions and eyes, including all confusion and fears. I denounce the noose around the neck, the fear of choking and any spirit that causes difficulty in breathing. I denounce the effects of all pagan objects and symbolism, aprons, books of rituals, rings and jewelry. I denounce the entrapping of others, and observing the helplessness of others during rituals. I denounce false communion, all mockery of the redemptive work of Jesus Christ on the cross, all unbelief, confusion and deception, and all worship of Lucifer as god. I humbly ask for your forgiveness, Lord Jesus, and for your blood to cleanse me of all the sins I have committed. Please purify my spirit, soul, mind, emotions and every other part of my body. Please destroy any evil spirits that have attached themselves to me, or my family, because of these sins and cleanse us with the fire of your holy spirit. I invite you into my heart, Lord Jesus, and enthrone you as my Lord and savior for all eternity. Amen.

Closing of Deliverance Prayers
Thank you, Lord Jesus, for awakening my sleeping spirit and bringing me into your light. Thank you, Lord, for transforming me by the renewing of my mind. Thank you, Lord, for pouring out your spirit on me, and revealing your word to me. Thank you, Lord, for giving your angels charge over me in all my ways. Thank you for my faith in you and that from my innermost being shall flow rivers of living water. Thank you for directing my mind and heart into the love of the father and the steadfastness of all your

ways. Fill me to overflowing with your life and love, my Lord and King, Jesus Christ. Amen.

Prayer for the Healer
Lord, Jesus, thank you for sharing with me your wonderful ministry of healing and deliverance. Thank you for the healing I have experienced today. I realize that the sickness of evil is more than my humanity can bear, so I ask that you please cleanse me of any sadness, negative thinking or despair that I may have picked up during my intercession for others. If during my ministry I have been tempted to anger, impatience or lust, cleanse me of those temptations, and replace them with your love, joy and peace. If any evil spirits have attached themselves to me or oppressed me in any way, I command you, spirits of earth, fire, water, the netherworld, or the evil forces of nature, to depart now and go straight to Jesus Christ, for him to deal with you as he wills. Come holy spirit, renew me, fill me anew with your power, your life and your joy. Strengthen me where I feel weak and clothe me with your light. Fill me with your life. Lord Jesus, please send your holy angels to minister to me and protect me from all forms of sickness, harm and accidents. I thank you and praise you my Lord, God and King. Amen.

Spiritual Warfare Prayer
Lord Jesus, I ask you today to cover me and my family, the whole world, especially our military and our priest, with your precious blood and protection. Uncover any hidden plot of the enemy before it has a chance to take root or effect or do any harm. Alert us to any hidden plots against us and provide in advance a peaceful solution to any damage the enemy tries to do. Bind and make mute any evil spirits that try to manifest or attach themselves to us in any way. We ask you to please hide from the enemy the

personal plans and ministries you have for us, so he has no access or knowledge of them. Let no weapon formed against us be able to prosper. In the name of Jesus Christ, I rebuke any curses, hexes, or spells sent against us. I bind all interplay, interaction and communication of evil spirits, and I claim the protection of the shed blood of Jesus Christ on _____. I ask you, Lord, to please send St. Michael, the Archangel, to drive out all the evil spirits who roam the earth and give St. Michael the authority to send all evil spirits straight to the recesses of hell, where they will remain forever. Lord Jesus, I also ask you to please let the waters of our baptism flow back through our bloodlines to cleanse us of any evil or unwanted tendencies or traits that we may have inherited from our ancestors. And lastly, Lord, I ask you to please bless my enemies by sending your holy spirit to lead them to repentance and conversion. We thank you, Lord, and we praise you Lord, for your boundless mercy and protection. Amen.

Simple Binding Prayer (Can be said Everyday)
Evil spirit, I bind you in the Name of Jesus Christ, and command you to go to the foot of the cross.

Simple Binding Prayer 2
Father God, I thank you for sending your son Jesus to die for me, and resurrecting him to sit at your right hand in Heaven right now. I thank you for bestowing upon him all power and authority over evil. In the name of Jesus Christ, I speak to any evil spirits, especially spirits _____, I bind you from attacking me now and throughout this day. Leave me now and go straight to Jesus Christ who will deal with you. I am covered and protected by the blood of Jesus Christ. Amen.

Scripture for Spiritual Warfare

Ephesians 6:10-18:10--Finally, my brethren, be strong in the Lord, and in the power of his might. 11-Put on the whole armor of God, that ye may be able to stand against the wiles of the devil. 12-For we wrestle not against flesh and blood, but against principalities, against powers, against the rulers of the darkness of this world, against spiritual wickedness in high places. 13-Wherefore take unto you the whole armor of God, that ye may be able to withstand in the evil day, and having done all to stand. 14-Stand therefore, having your loins girt about with truth, and having on the breastplate of righteousness; 15-And your feet shod with the preparation of gospel of peace; 16-Above all, taking the shield of faith, wherewith ye shall be able to quench all the fiery darts of the wicked. 17-And take the helmet of salvation, and the sword of the spirit, which is the word of God: 18-Praying always with all prayer and supplication in the spirit, and watching thereunto with all perseverance and supplication for all saints; To remove attachments: In Jesus's name, I reject all known and unknown agreements and contracts with this energy; I reject and banish this energy from (name of the attacked person)

A Poetic Verse (Especially effective for healers):

"May God be resurrected and his foes vanish. As wax melts before fire, as smoke is dispersed by the wind, so may all who hate the Lord flee from his sight, and the just rejoice!" "In God's name, I command all attached beings and spirits to leave this person in peace and unharmed never to return" in Jesus name Amen.

WICCAN/WHITE MAGIC SPELLS & CHANTS

Many of the spells and chants of Wiccan beliefs have other aspects that complement the spell or chant. Symbols are often used as well as candles, crystals, and incense in conjunction with the spoken word. To truly perform the spells in their most effective fashion, you need to become more educated in the Wiccan beliefs and ceremonies involved.

Protection Spell
This spell is to protect from the hate of another and can be done during any phase of the moon. Must have something that is connected to the person such as: piece of handwriting, picture, hair etc. Place this item in a container and set it aflame. Chant "away from me, away from me, away from me, away from me, away from me". This will not keep them away but will help establish a friendlier relationship with the person.

Another protection spell
"By the dragon's light, on this (current month) night, I call to thee to give me your might, by the power of thee, I conjure thee, to protect all that surrounds me, So mote it be, so mote it be!!"

Knights Protection Spell
Cast a circle on the ground all *casters* enter. The more *casters*, or people, involved - the more powerful. "Hear me Knights of past, Knights of the ancient law. Hear me dead Knights of an English tongue. Hear me Knights lost in battle, who's blade did good. Hear me Knights of old, hear me Knights of lost souls. This night I invoke thee. I summon thee to my arms aid. Hear me Knights, a new cause be given. Your body gone now spirit be. Hear me dead Knights I invoke thee. By your spirit blade I invoke

you. By your might I invoke you. By your spirit I invoke you. Come now follow a new cause, I summon thee. Each of thee I enlist. I invoke you dead Knights lost. Hear me and come to my aid. Hear me and fight at my side. Protect me from spirits harm. Fight my battles I say to thee. Hear me spirits of lost Knights, come to my aid, come to my side. Protect me from spirits harm. Protect me from spirits light. I invoke you. I invoke you. I invoke you. I invoke you. I invoke you. Let my army be done. Let it be. Let it be."

Simple Protection Chant
If you feel afraid at any time just say the following: "I walk in circles of light that nothing may cross." As you say it envision bright white light all around you.

Spell to Protect Yourself
"Elements of the sun, Elements of the day, Come this way, Powers of night and day, I summon thee, I call upon thee, to protect me. So shall it be."

The Binding of All Harm
There is a process involved with most binding spells which should be performed for best effect. Chant three times the following- "I bind all harm which might come to me. I bind it onefold, twofold and three. This that I wish so mote it be!"

SYMBOLS OF PROTECTION

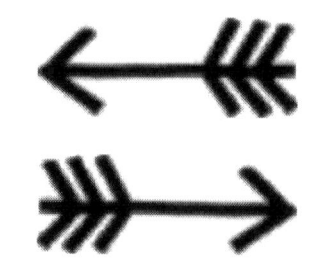

Arrows: A reliable tool of protection in Native American tribes, the arrow has come to symbolize the protection from and warding off evil. A symbolic arrow pointed left indicates the warding off of evil while an arrow pointed right invokes protection.

The Pentacle: a five-pointed star with the single point in the upward position is a symbol of light, positive power and protection. The Pentagram, which is an inverted Pentacle with the two points in the upward position and the single point downward, was introduced into the lexicon in the 1800s and came to represent darkness and Satanism.

In the Wiccan religion, the five points of the star are symbolic of the five elements (Earth, Fire, Water, Air, and Spirit) with each element representing a metaphysical trait:

Earth (lower left point) = Endurance
Fire (lower right point) = Courage
Water (upper right point) = Intuition and emotion
Air (upper left point) = Intelligence
Spirit (top point) = The divine

Triquetra: Used by Christians as a symbolic representation of the Holy

Trinity; God the Father, God the Son, and The Holy Spirit. The Triquetra is also used by Wiccans to symbolize protection. It is also known as the Trinity Knot which is symbolic of the three relationship vows (love, honor, and protect).

Algiz Rune: A powerful rune of higher vibration representing the divine might and plan of the universe and overall higher spiritual awareness. It is believed that through the energy of Algiz life feels sacred and through alignment with the divine a person becomes sacred and blessed by divine protection. The symbol represents man reaching toward the heavens and communicating with the gods and other entities throughout the universe.

The Eye of Ra: Symbolic of a mythological Egyptian being who functions as the female counterpart/goddess to Ra, the Sun God. The Eye goddess represents the maternal/sibling/consort/daughter of Ra and controls violent forces that can subdue Ra's enemies (agents of disorder that threaten his rule). Today, the symbol of the Eye of Ra is thought to bring wisdom and prosperity (monetary and spiritual wealth) to those who adorn it.

Cross: One of the oldest amulets, this symbol once belonged to the pagan population of Europe and western Asia centuries before Jesus walked the earth. Eventually it became a symbol of the Christian faith during the religious appropriation phase at the height of Christianity. The cross symbolizes the power of faith in casting out evil. Catholics cross themselves, invoking the power of the Holy Trinity as they do, for protection from the Devil and misfortune. The wearing of a silver cross is said to protect one from evil spirits and demonic activity.

The Helm of Awe: A Viking symbol of protection. Warriors would often carve this symbol into their protective garments or physically adorn their bodies with the symbol, usually placing in on their foreheads using blood, saliva, or lead. The Helm of Awe was thought to induce fear in the enemy thus providing the wearer protection. It was also thought to provide protection from illness and can be found in Norse medical manuscripts dating back to the 16th Century.

CRYSTALS & SEMI PRECIOUS STONES

Crystals and semiprecious stones were created when the earth was formed. For centuries people have developed a relationship with crystals and have noticed varied results. Some people believe that crystals and semiprecious stones have their own vibration which is believed to affect the physical, emotional, mental, psychological, and spiritual levels of being. Some people believe crystals contain "beings" or "guardian spirits" who are willing to cooperate with the programming of the crystal. Many people meditate with their crystals to be better "in tune" with the crystals' vibration.

Crystals have been found to be efficient absorbers and transmitters of energy. Some are better used for healing while others are better used for protection. Some people use crystals to work on their aura, to heal/balance chakras, or in combination with spells/rituals. Crystals also correspond to body parts and organs as well as the signs of the Zodiac. Some use crystals/stones as a divinatory tool, somewhat like Tarot cards. Each stone/crystal represents a set of traditional meanings. Obviously, there is not enough room in this book to go into great depth, but the basics will be covered and the crystals best used for protection will be included.

Crystals and stones should be chosen, cleansed, dedicated, programmed, charged, and stored properly. It is best to research and, if possible, learn from someone who works with crystals to get the greatest results.

Cleaning, Care, Storage and Programming

Cleaning
Due to a crystal's ability to absorb energy, most crystals need to be cleaned. As with most other things in life, there are always exceptions to the rule. Some crystals never need cleaned. Some are more fragile and need to be handled more delicately. Some are water soluble such as Selenite and should not get wet. This can be done by holding under running water, rinsing it off in the sea, or with salt water. As you physically clean the crystals focus on the negativity being washed away and the crystal being reenergized. Some crystals clean others such as Carnelian. If you store Carnelian with the other crystals cleaning will not be needed.

Selection, Charging, Storage
If possible, handle as many crystals/stones as you can before you purchase to be able to choose the one with the strongest vibration to you. It is best if you can put your hands into a bin of crystals until one sticks to your fingers. Make sure you always cleanse the crystal before use. Setting the crystals out in the sunlight or moonlight for a few hours will help recharge them. Some crystals should not be in direct sunlight due to the possibility of starting a fire (Quartz) or because the sunlight can damage them (Amethyst). Some crystals/stones charge other crystals/stones. Crystals and stones should be stored properly. Tumbled stones can be in a velvet bag together whereas natural crystals/stones can be easily damaged or scratch others. Be careful what you store together as some crystals/stones cancel each other out.

Programming and Dedication
Crystals should also be dedicated and programmed to the purpose you plan to use them for. Dedicate the crystal as

soon as it is cleansed to help focus the crystals inherent energy. Hold the crystal in your hand and imagine white light surrounding it. Say out loud, "I dedicate this crystal to the highest good of all. May it be used in light and love." To program the crystal, hold the crystal in your hands and let yourself be open to guidance of a higher power. Picture white light surrounding the crystal and be specific in your programming. Once you feel you are in tune with the crystal – feeling its unique vibration – then you say out loud "I program this crystal for ____". Leave the crystal in the open where you can see it or keep it in your pocket. It is helpful to hold it 2-3 times a day and the programming may need to be repeated periodically.

Crystal/Stone Types and Uses

Quartz
One of the most powerful healing and energy amplifier. Quartz cleanses other stones also.

Smoky Quartz aids in grounding spiritual energy, raising vibration levels during meditation, and eliminates EMF pollution leaving positive energy in its place.

Black Tourmaline
The one crystal that I make sure every team member has with them during investigations. It protects against EMF pollution, psychic attack, spells or ill-wishes. It protects and absorbs negative energy and releases toxic energy from emotions, mind, and body. Particularly effective against demonic entities.

Amethyst
Amethyst is an extremely powerful and protective stone with high spiritual vibration. It's known to open intuition and enhance psychic gifts. It is like black tourmaline in that it protects against EMF pollution and protects against psychic attacks.

Fire Agate
Offers a strong shield of protection, dispels fear, and transmutes energy. It is believed this stone returns harm back to its source.

Moonstone
Historically used for protection to travelers it is believed this stone protects during dark times. Used to enhance psychic abilities and helps develop clairvoyance. Calms the emotions and encourages lucid dreaming.

Black Jade
A stone of protection, its strong elemental energy shields not only the physical body, but guards against negative forces or entities, energy vampires, and people projecting anger and aggression.

Aegirine
Activates a strong, protective energy, guarding the aura and physical body, as well as fortifying the spirit in times of difficulty. Promotes wholeness and healing. powerful protector of those suffering jealousy, malice, mental influence or psychic attack from others. Expands the power of other stones related to healing.

Aqua Aura Quartz
Increases psychic skills and awareness. Strengthens meditation, enhances telepathy, clairaudience, clairvoyance, and psychic healing. It can be used as strength against psychic attacks as well. It can strengthen the auric field which is the first line of defense against negative psychic energy. It can protect against the psychic vampires and other parasitic or draining negative energies.

Peridot
Used for protection and cleansing. It helps you stay clear of people with bad influences on you or to minimize their influence. Helps deal with powerful emotions such as: guilt, stress, depression, anger, and jealousy.

Lapis Lazuli
A protective stone that contacts spirit guardians, recognizes psychic attack, blocks it, and returns the negative energy to the source.

Charoite:
A rare stone that comes from Russia, considered a guardian crystal. Said to enhance psychic awareness and abilities and acts as a catalyst for discovering and healing hidden fears.

Celestite
Stone with high vibration which serves as a communication tool for linking with the angels, Urges you toward enlightenment and spiritual development. Useful for stimulating clairvoyant communication, dream recall, and out-of-body experiences.

Hematite
Effective at grounding and protecting. Protects the soul and grounds it to the body, dissolves negativity and prevents negative energies from entering your aura.

ANIMAL SPIRIT GUIDES

With the belief that the spirit world is another dimension that exists alongside our own material world comes the belief that that world is populated by non-physical beings or "spirits".

These are thought to include ancestors, archangels, ascended spiritual masters, religious figures, deceased loved ones, fairies, and spirit animals.

The term "spirit guide", "helping spirit" or "guardian spirit" is used to describe spiritual beings that help in a life-positive way. People call on them for guidance, protection, healing, encouragement, and inspiration.

Humans have an intimate connection with animals in this world. There are the wild and domesticated varieties but there is also animal symbolism everywhere. We give our children stuffed teddy bears. The stock market is referred to as a "bull" or "bear" market. Politics are symbolized by the donkey and the elephant. Sports teams (Philadelphia Eagles), various organizations (Lions Club), historical fairy tales/children's stories, animal metaphors.

Christianity, the prevalent religion of this country, has maintained two totem animals, these being the fish and the lamb.
Shamans believe that everyone has power animals - animal spirits which reside within everyone, adding to their power and protecting them from illness; acting similarly to a guardian angel. Each power animal that you have increases your power so that illnesses or negative energy cannot enter your body.

The spirit also lends you the wisdom of its kind. Example, A hawk spirit will give you hawk wisdom, and lend you some of the attributes of hawk.

Receiving Messages from the Spirit World

We receive messages from the spirit world in four different ways – *Visual, Auditory, Kinesthetic, and Cognitive.*

Visual
To see an animal three times or more in a short period of time, or to have an unusual encounter with an animal. Also by *clairvoyance* – to see the spirit animal in the mind's eye – a vision or a vivid dream.

Auditory
Hearing the voice of a spirit animal in your mind giving you advice *(clairaudience)* or an environmental noise that triggers the thought of a certain animal. Also includes overhearing a conversation about an animal whether in person, TV, or radio.

Kinesthetic
This is when you feel or sense something. Also called a "gut feeling" or intuition. *Clairsentience* is feeling or sensing the ethereal form of the spirit animal or power animal and understanding what they are trying to communicate to you.

Cognitive
This is "knowing" also called insight or inspiration. *Claircognizance* is when a spirit animal or power animal communicates with you by generating a thought or thought process.

Calling on a Spirit Animal Guide

Since this chapter deals with protection you will need to know how to call on a spirit animal guide. Prayer, meditation, contemplation, and shamanic journeying are methods used to call on your guide. Once you have called on your guide you may get immediate results but more likely you will get further guidance and direction or ways to bring out more of that animal's characteristics you may want to exhibit.

Spiritual Protection
Ladybug, Ostrich, Peacock, Penguin, Shark, Swallow, and Wolf.

Emotional and Psychic Protection
Armadillo, Crab, Echidna (spiny anteater), Goose, Hawk, Horse (white), Hummingbird, Ladybug, Lynx, Mockingbird, Penguin, Porcupine, Rhinoceros, Seal, Shark, Swallow, Turtle, Whale, and Wolf.

Physical Protection
Blue Jay, Goose, Hawk, Ladybug, Mockingbird, Penguin, Shark, Weasel, and Wolf.

Protection from all Harm
Bear, Dog, Dragon, Gorilla, Jackal, Leopard, Polar Bear, Rhinoceros (black), Shark, Weasel, Wolf, and Woodpecker.

Notice Wolf and Shark are present in all 4 protection categories, Penguin is in 3 of the 4.

These last two groups are not so much for protection as is for developing psychic skills which of course is helpful when dealing with spirits or whatever else you may find while investigating.

Psychic Skills
Dolphin, Lemur, Moose, Scorpion, Whale

Psychic and Intuitive Development
Bobcat, Dolphin, Grebe (waterbird), Jaguar, Lemur, Magpie, Mole, Puffin, Scorpion, Sloth, Whale

HERBS & INCENSE

For thousands of years people have used smoke to send prayers up to: The Gods, Heaven, or whatever the main character is of the preferred religion or belief system. Herbs, plants, and flowers have been used for incense, aromatherapy, washes/spells, rituals/ceremonies, and medicines/food throughout history. Different plants have different strengths or uses attributed to them. The attributes differ depending upon belief system.

There are different ways to use these special plants. In dry form, they can be made into either incense to burn or ground up into a powder to be used in many different applications. Some are ground up wet to extract the natural oils or left in specific places for specific reasons – such as under the bed to keep nightmares away. Some are hung above doors or windows for specific reasons.

Listed below are herbs, plants, and flowers which are useful regarding paranormal investigation and protection. You can buy commercially produced incense however it is typically made with synthetic ingredients. Some people feel that synthetic components have little to no magical value. Again, it's a matter of what works best within a person's belief system.

Herbal Usage

Rosemary
Protection, love, lust, mental powers, exorcism, purification, healing, sleep, youth. Burn to purify and cleanse. Use in love and lust incenses and potions. Use for healing of all kinds. A tea of rosemary causes the mind to be alert.

Sage
Immortality, longevity, wisdom, protection, prosperity. Burn to purify and cleanse, often used as incense during sacred rituals. Commonly used in cleansing ceremonies which will be addressed in a later chapter. Especially good when moving into a new home.

Mistletoe
Burn as incense in your fireplace or a bonfire in your yard to repel any evil or negative energies in or around your home and property. In medieval times, mistletoe was hung over the door to keep demons from entering the home. This was also done to prevent lightning from striking the home. It may sound funny but in other times it was hung over to the door to attract love. It has been used in the past to chase sickness away. If bad dreams are keeping you awake, especially if caused by spirits lingering around, place mistletoe under the bed.

Aloe
Protection against illness.

Angelica
For banishing evil spirits and negative energies.

Asafetida
Perhaps the strongest banishing herb there is but it smells horrid especially when burned.

Basil
Makes a good floor wash or sachet for general protection.

Bay Leaf
General protection.

Bay Laurel
General protection.

Betony
Protects against negative energies and is good to protect against psychic attacks.

Birch
Protection from spirits.

Cactus
Banishing on both the physical and spiritual levels.

Celandine
Removes negative energies.

Cinnamon
Good general protection from negative energies.

Clove
General protection.

Comfrey
General protection, also good for protection when traveling in the astral realm.

Coriander
General protection.

Dandelion
Protects from bad dreams.

Dill
Good for protection against psychic attacks and as a general protection for babies.

Dragonsblood
Very strong protection against all evils.

Elecampane
Cleanses the area of negative energies.

Fern
General protection.

Garlic
Banishes all types of evil.

Hawthorn
General protection.

Heather
One of the better general protection plants, very pretty and easily grown in flower beds for extra protection.

Holly
Protection from lightening and evil.

Hyacinth
Protects against nightmares. Burn hyacinth incense before bed to help keep the nightmares at bay.

Hyssop
General protection.

Ivy
Good protection from psychic attacks and to keep unwanted guests from showing up.

Lavender
Protection against bad dreams.

Marjoram
Makes a good floor wash for general home protection.

Mullein
Strong general protection.

Nettle Leaves
Good protection against psychic attacks and to remove negative energies.

Onion
Protection against illness and evil.

Pennyroyal
Protection from psychic attacks and magic attacks from others.

Peony
General protection.

Rue
Banishes evil.

St. John's Wort
General protection.

Solomon's Seal
General protection.

Thistle
Protection against thieves.

Vervain
General protection.

Yarrow
Protection from psychic attacks and magic attacks.

ELEMENTS & MINERALS

Salt

prosperity, protection, purification, consecration of ritual tools. Virtually a universal purifier. Salt has been highlighted in nearly every spiritual belief system. Some ancient rituals call for pouring dry salt into a container of water to symbolize the dissolving of evil. Wiccans use a sprinkle of salt in water for blessings. Some ceremonial magicians use salt circles either for protection or to contain energy within a sacred space. Many people sprinkle a few grains around their sacred space to clear it of any unpleasant spiritual presences. Some people put blessed salt in all four corners of the home for protection.

The bible is full of references to the sanctity of salt. The bible references holy salt: "Covenants of salt" are mentioned in Num 18:19, referring to its indestructibility. "And he went forth unto the spring of the waters, and cast the salt in there, and said, 'Thus saith the Lord, I have healed these waters; there shall not be from thence any more death or barren land." 2 Kings 2:21 (King James Version)

Salt has long been a cure for many diseases, especially in times when disease was thought to be caused by malicious spirits. In ancient times, when babies were born, they were rubbed with salt to protect them from evil and possession of demons. The tradition of salt, the protector and purifier, stretches back as far as human memory, no doubt linked to salt's natural ability to preserve, purify, and even cure.

Holy Water
Used for protection and for blessings of purity. Holy Water is traditionally used by Christians during baptism ceremonies, for blessings of people, places, or things, and to repel evil.

Priests use it during exorcisms.

Often people are blessed with holy water sprinkled on them in the sign of the cross in conjunction with a blessing. Sometimes blessed salts are dissolved in holy water to intensify the effect.

Any portal/entryway (mirrors, windows, doors, etc.) can be blessed with holy water for protection as well.

Anointing Oil
Place olive oil in a small vial, pray a blessing over the oil, and store at room temperature.

UV Light
Ultraviolet light is a natural sterilizer, and is also used for protection against demons and evil spirits.

Iron
Used to protect against witches, evil spirits, and faeries. You normally need to place iron by doors and windows, like horseshoes above the main entrance, to keep the bad spirits away. You can also put an iron amulet under steps of main entrance to your home.

Silver
Works well on the paranormal and mystical spirits. Some claim that is due to silver being linked to the moon. The purity of this metal and its ability to enhance everyone's psychic strength. Silver has been used in many types of

paranormal creatures as well such as: vampires, werewolves, boogeymen, hexes and witches. It is also said to keep the newly dead from rising when silver nails are used in coffins. Silver, however does not work on ghosts like Iron does.

Jewelry and Adornments
Certain jewelry is a must have such as a St. Michael or St. Benedict medal, both of which can be worn on a necklace for protection.

How to Make Holy Water

1. Get some water. It doesn't matter if it is tap, purified, or regular bottled water.
2. Put the water into a clean container such as a bowl.
3. Drop a pinch of Kosher sea salt into it.
4. Recite Psalm 103 several times.

How to Use Holy Water

Bless yourself
This suggestion is obvious, but if we are only blessing ourselves with holy water on Sunday, then aren't we missing out on the rest of the week? You can never have too much grace or blessing in your life. Use holy water daily. Keeping a holy water font in the home is a great idea so that you, your family, and guests can be blessed in the comings and goings from your home. Keep the font right by the front door to ensure you never leave home without it.

Bless your house
If you haven't taken the time to bless your house with holy water, then no time is better than the present. Your home is the domestic Church and needs spiritual protection. You can sprinkle holy water in your home yourself, or have a priest formally bless your home using holy water as part of the house blessing ceremony.

Bless your family
Use holy water to pray and make the Sign of the Cross over your spouse and children before they go to sleep at night. Bonding the family to each other and to God in this way is a great family tradition to adopt. Keep a holy water bottle by the bedside for this purpose.

Bless your work space
If you work outside of the home, sprinkling your work space with holy water is a great idea, not only for spiritual protection on the work front, but also as to sanctify your daily work for the glory of God.

Bless your car
The car is probably the most dangerous place where you spend a significant amount of time each day. Never underestimate the power of holy water applied to your vehicle to keep you safe from harm's way, when used in faith and trust in God. In fact, you can also have a priest bless your car with holy water.

Bless your vegetable garden
It was a common practice in the Middle Ages for people to sprinkle their vegetable gardens with holy water. In times when people were very dependent on crops for their livelihood, lack of rain or early frosts could be devastating. Using holy water to bless and sanctify the plants that would

be used for the family's sustenance showed their reliance on God's grace.

Bless the sick
If you know of any sick friends or family, then blessing them with holy water probably counts as a corporeal *and* a spiritual work of mercy. If you visit the sick in a hospital or nursing home, bless their living space with holy water and leave a holy water bottle with them as a comfort in their time of need.

Bless your pets
Many parishes on the feast of St. Francis of Assisi have a rite of blessing for pets. Pets are loved companions for individuals and families and often provide a great service to them, and even these can be blessed with holy water because all creation has the end of giving glory to God. This also applies to livestock and farm animals that provide labor, livelihood, and nourishment to humans.

Here is a simple prayer to say when using holy water:

"By this holy water and by Your Precious Blood, wash away all my sins, O Lord. Amen."

How to make anointing oil

1. Obtain olive oil. You can use plain olive oil but Extra-virgin cold-pressed oil is the purest that you can find in most grocery stores.
2. Put oil in a small bottle or vial.
3. Pray this blessing over the oil:

"God, I pray that you anoint this oil in your name. I pray to you that you cleanse it of any defilement in or upon it, and that you make it Holy for the work of your glory. May this oil be done in the name of the Father, The Son and the Holy Spirit. Amen.

How to use anointing oil

To perform an anointing on yourself or others, draw a cross on your forehead while saying: *"In the name of the Father, and the Son and the Holy Spirit. Amen."*

To use the anointing oil in your house, walk into each room and make the sign of the cross in oil on each door frame. As you do so, pray that God fills your house with the Holy Spirit and that everything that happens from now on will be done in according to the Father's will.

CANDLES & SPIRIT GUIDES

Candles can be used for protection also, you can use any shape or size. The best colors to use are, in order of spiritual preference: Purple-for higher guidance and protection, White-for higher guidance and protection, Yellow-used for mental pursuits, Blue-used for spiritual pursuits. Black-used in rituals to protect and ward off evil.

It does not matter if your candle is scented or not, unless you find the scent distracting, if so use an unscented candle. Many people use the little menorah candles that can be found in Kosher section of most grocery stores. They are small, white, unscented, and burn quickly for use in spells.

As you focus on the flame, imagine yourself in a quiet place. You may have a favorite place or somewhere you loved to go as a child that was quiet and secluded.

Bring that place to mind and focus on it. It can be anything ranging from sitting under a tree to bring an Egyptian temple (my personal favorite) or anything in between. Just make sure that whatever you're imagining includes only you and your surroundings.

If you're imagining your old tree house you had as a kid, don't also imagine all your childhood friends there with you. As soon as you have your ideal quiet place in mind, gently send out your intention by saying "I wish to contact my spirit guide".

Focus again on the flame if you find your mind is wandering. Don't stop, just re-focus on the flame and continue. **It is crucial that you say this simple invocation for Protection:**

"O holy Mother/Father God (*Jesus, Mary, Isis, whomever you wish*) I ask for your protective white light to surround me and my home. I ask for your protection now. I open my heart, mind, and spirit to any knowledge sent to me by spirits or angels of the light. Only beings of light shall be allowed to enter my sacred space. No being of negative or mal intent can enter. I open myself to my spirit guides and angels. As I ask for their guidance and advice now."

Once your spirit guide appears, introduce yourself, even though they already know who you are, it never hurts to use good manners. Then ask them who they are. Wait for a name. One will be provided. Tell yourself you will remember the name so you can write it down once your session is over.

Next ask your spirit guide if he/she has any advice to impart to you now. Many times, for this first visit, the spirit guide simply makes their presence known and won't have a message for you. If that is the case, do not despair. Next time you contact your spirit guide they will have something of importance to say. Once your spirit guide has imparted their message, be sure to thank them and then will yourself back to your normal state of consciousness.

OUIJA BOARDS

There are certain rules you should follow when dealing with a Ouija board.

One is that you should never use it in your house. Another is to never allow the planchette to move forwards or backwards through every letter of the alphabet or every numbers as this is allegedly trick the demon Zozo uses to escape the board. I will leave it to you to research the history of the board and the various trappings that come with it including that viability of the existence of Zozo.

Closing out the session

Regardless of your belief in the mystic oracle that is a Ouija board. there is one rule that should be observed above all others: ensure the planchette hits "Goodbye" before ending your session.

Failure to do so may lead to unintended consequences such as an angry spirit overstaying its welcome. If while using the board you encounter a dark entity, sever the connection with the Ouija board immediately. Tell the spirit you no longer wish to speak with it. If it refuses, force the planchette to "Goodbye" yourself then remove the planchette from the board.

This should break the connection and the Ouija board should be "closed." Store it by wrapping the planchette in cloth, separate from the board. Then, put them together in a safe place.

Removing or Ridding the Board

Depending on your belief or personal experience with the Ouija board, you may be left with the desire to get rid of it. There are accepted means of distancing yourself from the board.

Never burn it. That releases the spirit from the board and in doing so would mean you'd be haunted forever. Instead, if you'd like to get rid of the Ouija board entirely, take it to holy ground or graveyard and bury it in the ground with blessed salt, holy water, and Saint Michael medals. Remember to keep the board and the planchette separated. Sprinkle the ground above with Holy Water and blessed salt, then apply the medals and end with a binding prayer. Make sure to cleanse the areas where you used the board.

Despite all of this, some claim that once a connection with the spirit world is made, it can never be broken. Your fate, from the moment you use a Ouija board, is bound to the other side. I would never suggest using a Ouija board or be in the presence of someone using one as there are too many evil spirits and demons connected to them.

CHAPTER 3: THE EVOLUTION OF GHOST HUNTING EQUIPMENT

The world of paranormal investigations has been around since the first ghost story was uttered. Humankind has long been occupied with figuring out what happens when we shuffle off our mortal coil. Do we go on in this world as spirits or do we move to an astral plane or an ethereal higher realm? Do we maintain the ability to communicate with the living or does the physical world find a way to move on without us?

As a higher thinking species, we have boundless questions when it comes to ghosts and other supernatural phenomena. In our pursuit to discover answers we eventually ushered in the age of the modern ghost hunter.

Today, paranormal investigators are armed with an arsenal of hi-tech equipment ranging from digital voice recorders and full-spectrum digital cameras/camcorders to Electromagnetic Field (EMF) detectors and FLIR thermal imaging devices.

With every advance in modern technology, ghost hunters always ask, "How can this benefit my research?"

The field of paranormal research is in a constant state of evolution, growing from its infancy as a "science" in the 1800s. With a limitless supply of knowledge now at our fingertips, we are smarter and better- educated than those early investigators who blazed the trail for us. That is not to disparage their contributions to the field, for without them we wouldn't be where we are today.

Life was a lot different when the first paranormal investigators came onto the scene. They had to work with what is now considered primitive and antiquated means, and producing quantifiable evidence wasn't as easy as it is now.

Let's look at the history of a paranormal investigator's tools and the progression to our modern set of tools. The road to our modern era of technology all began with...

Historical Investigator Equipment

Pencil and Paper
One of the most important tools any investigator should carry is a notepad and something to write with. In the dawn of the ghost hunter this was once the only item an investigator would carry. They would log dates, times, and locations of activity. They would notate naturally occurring phenomenon (Dog barking, people walking around in another room, voices outside) and use it as a baseline for when they logged inexplicable phenomenon (Scratching at the walls, doors slamming, furniture moving, etc...) Pencil and paper was truly the only way to document and keep a historical log of events. Additionally, since spirit writing (the process by which a spirit can communicate through a living host) was a big part of early investigations, always having paper and a writing instrument was a must if an investigator wanted to channel a spirit and allow them to write through their bodies.

Felt Overshoes
Most modern investigators don't give too much thought as to how they adorn their feet aside from agreeing that sneakers are the best bet as they make the least noise. When early investigators came about, society was a "dress up" culture. Men wore suits and women wore dresses when investigating and the sneaker wasn't a commonly worn shoe outside of athletics. Each investigator would bring with them a pair of felt overshoes, soft felt that slips over their dress shoes to lessen the impact of wooden soles on hard floors. With a quieter step, it was easier to hear paranormal activity and rule out noise contamination from the investigators.

Trigger Objects
Today, provoking a spirit into responding by yelling at it, challenging it or cursing at it is considered the sign of an amateur investigator and is generally frowned upon as a tactic. During the dawn of the industry however it was thought that this was the best way to prove the existence of ghosts. Because provocation was a common tactic, paranormal investigators of the past would bring trigger objects with them. If it was reported that the ghost died of poisoning, vials of poison would be brought to the scene and placed about the room. If the ghost was thought to be a child, a replica of their favorite toy would be displayed and the investigator would taunt the deceased with it.

Thermograph and Thermometers
Drastic and noticeable fluxes in temperature have long been linked to the presence of a paranormal entity. Whereas today we have infrared/laser thermometers capable of pulling a temperature out of thin air all within seconds, getting temperature readings of a room in the early days of investigations was a bit more cumbersome. Traditional thermometers and thermograph machines (machines used to track and document changes in temperature over a long period of time) were often used. These items were large, delicate, and time-consuming but were vitally important to the process.

Mercury
This element was quite a versatile tool for early investigators as they were able to use it to monitor changes in room temperature as well as to monitor tremors in the room which could indicate footsteps or other spiritual movement. It was also thought to be a useful tool in warding off evil spirits.

Dowsing/Divining Rods
Dowsing, or divining rods, were two L-shaped rods that could be held by the shorter arm of the L with the longer arms pointing outward in front of the investigator. The theory is that the rods can detect energy and when they do, the arms pointing out will cross. They were originally used to detect underground water sources but paranormal investigators appropriated the tool to detect energy put out by the presence of spirits. Investigators believed (some still do) that since spirits are pure energy that they could use the rods to detect and communicate with the dead using yes or no questions. The investigator would ask a question and for a positive response, the spirit would cross the rods, for a negative response they would leave the rods uncrossed. The use of dowsing rods is still a common practice for a lot of groups, though using the rods to validate claims of a haunting is divisive, with some claiming results can be skewed by human error/ignorance.

Stones
As previously discussed in the book, stones and gems play a significant role in the world of the paranormal. Some are conductive and absorb energy while other repel energy. Early investigators always kept a variety of stones in their possession to either draw in positive energy or rebuke negative energy. This practice is still common with some investigators though now they incorporate the stones into wearables instead of carrying around a satchel of rocks.

Ouija Boards
Now frowned upon by most investigators and often thought to be the source of a haunting, the Ouija board was once a tool of the trade for early paranormal investigators. It was used to communicate with the dead to gather as much information about the presence as possible. It was a novelty and the practice soon fell out of favor as the validity of

responses came into question. Investigators simply could not prove that they were not manipulating the board.

Contemporary Investigator Equipment

The advent of the technological age ushered in a renaissance of sorts within the paranormal community. Audio and video recording devices became more compact and sensitive, cameras moved from film to digital resulting in sharper images. Night Vision (Night Shot) moved from the military use into the civilian world and opened a new world of possibilities for investigators who could now record in low to zero light situations.

Being a paranormal investigator in the 21st century means that you have access to a variety of tools designed and engineered solely for you. Some tools started off as functional tools for different trades but were appropriated and re-engineered to meet the needs of ghost hunters.

If you are looking to begin your journey as a paranormal investigator, here are some basic pieces of equipment you will need to be a success:

Pencil and Paper
Yes indeed! What was true for our ancestors in the 1800s is still true to this day. Do not even contemplate going on an investigation without the means to take notes. You will use a pad and pencil (or pen) more than you can imagine. Log baseline readings, map the layout of a house/business, document times of occurrences, compile a list of questions for EVP (Electronic Voice Phenomenon) sessions, jot down notes of historical significance about the property. The uses for a notebook and writing tool are wide and varied and not having one in your possession just announces to everyone that you are an amateur.

Flashlights
You are going to be walking around unfamiliar buildings in the dark. Be sure to carry a flashlight with you and keep backup flashlights and plenty of batteries on hand.

Batteries:
Ghosts will not hesitate to use your battery power to draw energy. Battery drain is a common occurrence on investigations so it is wise to bring along a well-stocked backup supply of every kind of battery you use in your equipment. If you have camcorders and digital cameras, ensure you purchase and bring along fully charged backups for those devices as well. If you experience a battery drain, be ready, something is about to happen!

Digital Camera
You can get a 12-megapixel digital camera for cheap these days, so there is no excuse for not carrying one with you into an investigation. Ensure it has plenty of room for pictures (buy extra SD cards), a decent battery life, and functional flash. A simple point-and-shoot digital camera should be used in lieu of your cellphone camera.

Digital Camcorder
Nothing gets the old blood pumping more than catching video evidence that supports the claims of a haunting. Video is one of the best sources of the proof of the paranormal when captured legitimately. Prices run from relatively affordable to completely cost prohibitive depending upon the make and model. You don't need to go crazy and max out your Best Buy credit card. Some features you should look for are high storage capacity, low light recording, and a "steady" feature to help eliminate nausea-inducing shaky footage. If you want a camera designed specifically for ghost hunting, look at several online shops like www.ghoststop.com that create custom

cameras that operate in the full spectrum. If you opt to get a camcorder with night vision and full spectrum, you will need to purchase an addition IR/UV lamp to help for those videos shot in the dark.

Digital Voice Recorder
This modern take on the old-fashioned tape recorder started off as a tool for college students and boardroom meeting attendees, but seeing value in a compact device that records audio, it was soon in every paranormal investigator's toolkit. The digital voice recorder allows investigators to conduct EVP sessions whereby they ask any spirit who may be present a list of questions, pausing long enough after each question to allow an answer. The theory is that the answers, while not audible to the human ear, will be captured on the recording and can be heard upon playback. When you capture a great EVP, you will not regret your decision to purchase and carry one of these voice recorders.

Ambient Thermometer
If you aren't carrying one of these personally, someone on your team should have one. These compact digital thermometers quickly report surrounding air temperature and can detect when there is a sudden drop or increase in temperature. They are great for detecting cold spots which are believed to be created when a ghost manifests.

EMF Detector
An EMF detector is an electrician's tool that is used to detect electromagnetic output of electronic devices and electrical wiring in a home. The higher the reading the stronger the electromagnetic output. These can range greatly in style and ability from simple to complex, so shop around and find one that works for you. Most investigators are fond of the K-II (K2) meters that were featured heavily on shows like Ghost Hunters. The K-II is a simplistic EMF

detector that uses a set of lights that range from green to red (with orange and yellow filling the range between). Low level EMF is indicated by a green light. As you near a source with higher EMF output, the yellow, orange, and red lights will illuminate and the device will emit an audible tone that increases in pitch and speed as the EMF levels increase. The theory surrounding EMF and the paranormal is two-fold. It is believed that homes with high EMF fields attract ghosts and other spirits because it is a form of energy from which the spirits can draw to manifest and make their presence in our world known. The other theory is that humans are susceptible to the effects of high EMF fields and the side effects of being exposed to constant high EMF levels can mimic the sensation of a malevolent presence. People with EMF sensitivity can feel paranoid, disoriented, nauseous, and have their fight-or-flight response triggered. These physiological responses can make it feel like there is a malevolent spirit present. If an investigator enters a home and does an initial baseline reading of the house and determines there is a high level of EMF within the home, it might help disprove a haunting and give the homeowner some peace.

Two-Way Radio
Invest in a set of two-way radios. These are not child toys like walkie-talkies, they are hand held citizen-band radios with ranges up to several miles. Your team should have several sets, especially for larger investigation sites. You will pick a channel on the radio with no chatter and use that as your means of communication between teams and with the command center. A reliable set of two-way radios can set you back about $100.00.

There are a lot of other awesome tools that you can have in your arsenal, just expect to pay a lot of money. A lot of the products have gained popularity because of their use in paranormal programming, so the markup on these once affordable everyday tools has rendered them expensive. The K-II meter was once under twenty dollars and now retails for over fifty dollars.

Some items to consider would be motion detectors, full spectrum camera/camcorder with UV/IR lamp, and EMF pumps that actually pump electromagnetic fields into the air from which ghosts can draw energy to manifest.

Lastly, be wise, do not spend an exorbitant amount of money on your equipment until you are sure that you want to seriously commit to being an investigator. Start small and sensible and slowly add to your toolkit. Learn how to use each piece of equipment thoroughly to prevent false positives because of user error.

CHAPTER 4: PARANORMAL THEORIES AND BELIEFS

Theories and Beliefs

Paranormal Investigations, or "Ghost Hunting", is considered a pseudo-science or fringe science. It is made up almost entirely of unproven theories and every individual and group has their own theories on how and why things occur within the course of investigations. Despite the wide and varied array of theories floating around, there are some that are commonly accepted as truth or fact.

Relative Time to Object Theory
(aka the "Singapore Theory")
The Relative Time to Object Theory is sometimes known as the "Singapore Theory", though how that name came to be assigned to this theory in unknown to us.

In the "Relative Time to Object Theory" many investigators claim that paranormal activity will increase when objects such as old furniture, clothing, toys, music, etc. are brought into a location that used to house these objects during the object's specific period.

When the object is brought into the location the ghost that supposedly haunts the location will interact more, because the ghost can relate to the specific object.

For example; in the ballroom on the Queen Mary, if you play music that was played during ships era, paranormal activity may increase due to spirit familiarity with the music of those times.

To potentially increase paranormal activity in a historic location, consider introducing the following types of objects/ideas relative to the era of the property:

- Music
- Toys
- Furniture
- Dolls
- Clothing
- Food items
- Discuss Presidents/leaders of the time
- Discuss events pertinent to the era of the property

The Renovation Theory
The Renovation Theory states that when renovations are made to a home or business, paranormal activity will increase.
Home remodeling may trigger paranormal activity. There are some creepy stories that revolve around this idea. Even paranormal investigators noted that most of their personal encounters with the supernatural have occurred during periods of renovation. So, when people come to them to tell their spine-chilling experiences, there is one question these ghost experts ask at the beginning, "Have you recently started or completed remodeling your home?"

It may sound like a weird question, but it is very important for paranormal experts to know whether their clients did any home renovations because this can, believe it or not, instigate or heighten activities involving creatures of the third kind. Here are the two most common reasons why.

1. Home Remodeling May Disturb Sleeping Spirits

Renovations may cause a spirit to wake – as simple as that. This spirit may have been sleeping in your home for years. In most cases, the spirit is that of a past homeowner who doesn't want any changes made to what he or she believes to be his/her 'home.'

2. A Spirit May Take Offense to the Change in their Established Environment

Often, a ghost likes to stay in a comfortable environment since there are times when a ghost is angry or in a disordered state of mind. When their environment, which they are accustomed to, is suddenly changed due to home renovations, they become very uncomfortable. For spirits who haven't realized yet that they're already dead, the altered environment may appear chaotic to them. On the other side, ghosts who have grown accustomed to their usual surroundings may not like the sudden changes.

How to Prevent Paranormal Activity During Renovations

What can you do to get rid of furious spirits who don't agree with your remodeling 'their' home, which is 'yours'? Paranormal experts suggest the following:

1. Knock and bang loudly on doors while performing major home remodeling as this can disturb and eventually creep out spirits before they creep you out.
2. Offer incense to the spirits every morning before the renovation begins.
3. Have the laborers finish the work and leave the property just before the sun starts to set. Don't forget to lock up all the equipment cautiously.
4. Keep the lights on and bright, particularly the ones in every corner.
5. Keep the house clean, with no clutter and dust.
6. Turn the music player on and play happy, upbeat songs.
7. Since you're remodeling, put away those squeaky doors because they attract mad, hungry spirits more.

8. Before remodeling your home, announce: "You're not real. You're unable to hurt me. You can't influence me."

Stone Theory

Limestone, Quartz, and/or Magnetite deposits can supposedly retain an energy imprint from historical events and occurrences. When this imprint is released because of breakage, fracture, or movement, a residual haunting may occur.

Using Alternate Light Spectrums for Investigations Theory

The light we see is known as "white light" or "visible light". It's really a combination of all visible colors of the spectrum which is a small fraction of the overall Electromagnetic Spectrum.

The Electromagnetic Spectrum starts with long wave/low frequency light on the left side (which includes the infrared light, radar, FM/AM radio wavelengths, and television signals).

It is followed by the narrow section of "visible with the naked eye" white light and is followed by the right side of the spectrum that contains short wave/high frequency light such as Ultraviolet lights, X-Rays and Gamma Rays.

Yes, radio, television and radiation are all part of the same electromagnetic spectrum as visible light except that they are invisible to the naked eye.

The theory is that ghosts, spirits, and demons reside within the ultraviolet and infrared ends of the spectrum, rendering them invisible to the naked eye. As they move from one end of the spectrum to the other we might catch glimpses of them within the visible light.

Use of "Full Spectrum" cameras is believed to capture better results in the search for proof of a haunting as they can reveal the full spectrum and allow investigators to see into a once invisible world where perhaps ghosts dwell.

Air Ion Theories

An ion is an atom or molecule with a net electric charge because of gaining or losing one or more electrons. There are two commonly held theories that relate to ionization of the surrounding air within an environment.

Theory #1

If there is a ghost present, it may influence the ions in the air by disrupting the natural or manmade ion counts in the air.

Theory #2

When a ghost attempts manifestation it needs to absorb some form of energy to do so. By drawing either positive or negative ions out of the air the ghost may be able to manifest.

Some investigators invest in an ion pump to pump positive ions into the air within the environment and in theory provide fuel for potentially present spirits to manifest.

Ion Safety Warning:

Scientists have done studies of positive and negative ions and have discovered that negative ions have a positive effect on humans while positive ions have a negative effect.

Some of the side effects caused by a high positive ion count are as follows:

- Violent tendencies
- Depression
- Dizziness
- Chills
- Tremors
- Sleeplessness
- Fatigue
- Irritability
- Paranoia
- Nausea
- Lethargy
- Respiratory symptoms
- Headaches/migraine
- Increase in heart attacks
- High blood pressure
- Increase in optical disturbances
- Anxiety
- Body pains/aches etc...

Energy Loss Theory

All living things need some form of energy to move about and to be active. For example, humans eat food and store the energy that is in the food, so later they burn off the energy supply in whatever activities they are doing, such as walking jogging, etc. Plants take in the sunlight energy and carbon dioxide energy to photosynthesize.

In theory, some investigators believe that when a ghost is trying to manifest it will try to draw in any energy that is around the area. The ghost may try to draw energy from the investigators them self, causing them to suddenly feel nauseous or tired, or it may draw from the electrical power from your batteries that is in the equipment you are using. Many investigators claim that they will get sudden battery drainage from the digital camera, or video camera.

Mirror Gateway Theory

It is a centuries old belief that mirrors are portals to the other side, a gateway between worlds. They have been around for thousands of years in one form or another, and over time so many folktales and superstitions have been developed around them.

As far back as ancient times mirrors were used to scry; a common practice whereby mystics could see distant places, people, and timelines.

The Romans believed that to break a mirror would bring bad luck for 7 years.

There were also beliefs that the reflection bore the soul of the individual staring into it and that by studying their reflection one could gain insight into their true nature. It is possible that this belief gave rise to vampires not having a reflection as they would have no soul.

In the Jewish faith, it is important to cover all mirrors in a house where someone has died. If they are not covered the deceased's soul may enter a mirror and become trapped, unable to move on from this world into the afterlife.

Monks would place tiny mirrors on a small slender stick which they would slide up beside their nose so they could see spirits in the reflection using their peripheral vision.

Then we have newer urban legends like standing in front of a mirror and calling for Bloody Mary three times.

Many believe that mirrors can be used as a portal into our world by which ghosts and other entities can enter our home. Many reports have been made regarding antique mirrors and paranormal activity.

Some legends say that by gazing into a mirror while seated in dark room with nothing more than a lit candle, you will be able to to see spirits if they are present in your home. This idea is the basis for the Psychomanteum or Apparition Booth. This a darkened room with a series of mirrors set up in a specific way to allow the viewer to see, and even communicate with, spirits.

But what is it that gives the mirror this perceived power? Is there validity to all of this? I have, in my time as a paranormal investigator, had my share of strange occurrences with mirrors.

In one investigation of a family under siege by spirits, a great deal of activity had to do with an antique mirror in their bedroom.

The first thing to happen was, each time this malevolent spirit made its presence known there would come a heavy thump from the master bedroom. In one such instance, the homeowner, (who had taken to carrying a camera everywhere within the house) snapped several pictures of the master bedroom.

One photo containing an image of the mirror showed that the mirror beheld a strange scene within the reflection. Analysis of the image in the mirror revealed a woman in an old-style dress coming down an ornate staircase. Additionally, we could make out two open doors where stood a tall man in a black suit, his back to the scene. Lastly, we could make out a small child with a toy or doll looking up at the man in the doorway.

There was nothing within the bedroom that would produce such an inexplicable image within the mirror's reflective surface. Our first speculation was that the mirror was a doorway.

After a few months of research, I discovered a location that matched the reflected image in the mirror.

It is important to point out that haunting we were investigating was occurring in a townhome that once served as the servants' quarters for a grand old mansion. It was within this townhome that the mirror resided.

I contacted the owners of the mansion and was granted permission to visit the site. When I finally entered the mansion's main floor, there it was, the same grand staircase and the two doors as seen in the reflection of the mirror in the townhouse. It was an exact match.

How could a scene in a mansion located one thousand yards away play out in the mirror located in a second-floor bedroom of a townhouse?

Back in the townhouse I decided to conduct an experiment by covering the mirror with a thick black cloth in hopes of closing the doorway.

Funny thing about closing doorways, as the homeowner and I quickly learned; it is best to allow the spirit to leave first lest you end up sealing it inside the room with you. The spirit was most displeased as evidenced by the banging and clatter it made.

So, what is it about mirrors, (specifically older mirrors) that seems so attractive to spirits?

Most older mirrors have a silver metal coating on the back side of the glass surface and silver is a very interesting metal. It seems that silver atoms and their electrons are not densely packed. Electrons interact with light waves which cause the electrons to move and thus cause the light waves to reflect. Interestingly, the electrons can match the speed of the visible and slower infrared frequencies and reflect them back.

However, in the case of ultraviolet light frequencies, these are much too fast and pass through the mirror. Silver, which is used in a great deal of these mirrors, has the highest electrical and thermal conductivity of any metal on the periodic table and is one of the greatest optically reflective materials available. It also has the lowest contact resistance of all metals.

Remember, light is an electromagnetic field and silver is electrically conductive. This will cancel the field and cause the wave to reflect away from the mirror.

I have theorized for many years now that spirits have an electromagnetic field in the higher ultraviolet range of frequency. If this is the case, the conductivity of a silver backed mirror would be attractive as a doorway and the fact that if these spirits operate at higher UV frequencies, they would not cancel out, but rather pass through, the mirror with ease. Just a theory. We need a lot more experimentation to validate this one.

Ley Lines and Their Power

Ley lines are a spider web of invisible, yet subtle, measurable energy paths which wrap around the earth. Ley lines are also seen as "arteries" of the earth, "veins" of energy flow. There seems to be a boost of electromagnetic energy where two or more lay lines intersect. At these intersections, a power point is created which emanates out into a concentrated energy force. (Many of the important ancient monuments are built on these intersecting lines.)

Ley Lines are believed to elevate people's brainwaves and put them into an alpha state, which promotes healing.

Alpha brain waves are considered the relaxed brainwaves and associated with increased serotonin (the body's own happy drug), increased immune system function, balanced mood, production of higher creativity, increased problem-solving skills, and elevates learning ability.

Ley lines are also believed to be where the highest levels of paranormal activity occur. Because intersecting lines have such high energetic output, it gives spirits and ghosts enough power to cross between the realms of both worlds.

Ghost Can Harm You Theory

Can a ghost harm you? Yes, which is why ghost hunting is dangerous if you're not prepared or trained for what you're doing. Ignorance can result in you jeopardizing not only your safety, but the safety of others.

Possession is a risk a paranormal investigator faces when encountering a demon. Demons can pose as ghosts leading you to believe that you are dealing with a run-of-the-mill haunting. It is only when you're in the midst of everything you discover otherwise.

In many healing circles, the modern term for possession is Spiritual Attachment. Historically, when a possessed individual was released from the bonds of possession, it was called "depossession". The accepted contemporary term for this phenomenon is "Spiritual Attachment Release" or "Spiritual Attachment Release Therapy".

A Spiritual Attachment happens when a "non-crossed over" spirit (human, or inhuman), attaches itself to a living human or animal to use the energy of the living to exist, or worse yet, to intentionally manipulate the living's behavior for their own motivations.

An Attachment Spirit is a Spirit who does not exist in the Light and does not have a physical body, and as such they are without access to energy gained from food and water. They also do not have access to energy from Divine Source energy (like other, Divine Spirits do).

Spirits who are cut off from both physical energy and energy from a Divine Source (Heaven, the Light, whatever you want to call it) have few choices from which to cull the energy required to move and exist. They can choose to harness it from their local environment, or they can choose to directly tap into the energy of someone who is living.

As living being we have access to energy from both physical (food, water, sleep) and spiritual, Divine Sources. We gain energy from the food we eat, and we are also able to gain it from Source energy through our connection to the Light and to Mother Earth.

For Attachment Spirits, who are often very low on their own energetic resources, many humans appear to have a bounding and limitless supply of energy.

We also still have a physical body through which we can partake in physical activities – like driving, drinking alcohol, and eating, to name a few things that could motivate an ill intended Spirit to use your body or your energy for their own purposes.

When a Spirit chooses to Attach to a living human, it can happen for various reasons and to varying degrees.

Why Spirits Attach to People
There are 4 big reasons why a Spirit would want to attach themselves to a living human.

1. They've seen other Spirits do it and don't know another way to get energy

I've seen Spirits attach to people just because they didn't know another way. Perhaps because they are new to being Earthbound and they saw that the only way they could get Energy was to connect themselves to the energy of another person.

2. They feel that direct harnessing of energy from people is easier than gathering from the environment

Collecting energy from the environment tends to be more of a learned skill and requires more time and effort. Similarly, foraging for nuts and berries yourself is more challenging that just plopping yourself in someone else's strawberry field for dinner.

3. They still want to do the things they did when they were alive; particularly the case for addicts

This is especially the case for those that were addicted to substances or activities while they were alive. Only now, they're dead and do not have a physical body through which to experience the same highs they still want to experience.

So, these Spirits now connect themselves to someone who is already an addict of their choice, or someone who they think is vulnerable enough that it would be easy to make them into an addict. In doing this, the addict Spirit still gets to feel the high through the living person, whom they have now turned into an addict.

4. To intentionally manipulate behavior for the purposes of causing harm

Bad people who die yet do not cross over are still bad. They maintain the trappings of their human existence and continue in death the same behaviors they held in their living form. If they derived pleasure from manipulating and hurting others in the physical world, the will continue to do so in the spiritual realm.

These spirits can and will attach themselves to a vulnerable person strictly to cause harm and in some cases, the Spirit, who is already "dark," may want to bring the living person and those around them to "dark side," too.

Levels of Attachment
Humans are made of millions of energetic particles that comprise the molecules that form the backbones of our entire physical body and our own spirit. Our bones, blood, thoughts, and emotions are all made of energy.

These energetic particles produce tiny energetic fields and together they combine to form the human energy field, otherwise known as the aura.

We have a physical body – our blood, our bones, our skin and our brain.

We have a spiritual body – otherwise known as the human spirit. It comprises our emotions, thoughts, feelings, personality and experiences.

We have an energetic body – the energy that makes up our physical body and our spiritual body.

Generally, the spiritual body of a living human resides inside the physical body. Surrounding and encompassing those two, is the whole of the energetic body.

When a Spirit "attaches" to us, it can happen in these ways: They can simply attach to our energetic field in the way that a tether would be attached to a pole, or they can step completely inside a living person. When this happens, they can replace or push aside the Spirit of the actual living person. This is the more extreme version and it is what was once known as a full blown spiritual possession.

A person can also have more than one attachment. Either there are individual Spirits attached in multiple places, OR there's a single Attachment Spirit who themselves had attachments before they died, and went into the afterlife with spiritual attachments of their own. In cases like this, this person's spiritual attachments can become so cumbersome to them, that they can weigh someone down, preventing them from crossing over entirely. When this happens, the single attachment plus their attachments are all using the energy of the living person to whom they are all attached.

How it Happens
Attachments to the living occur only when there's a vulnerability present to do so. When your guard is down, when your feelings are low, and when you aren't the purest and happiest version of yourself this is when you may be unguarded. Unfortunately, times like this happen to everyone, making it possible for any person to be vulnerable and susceptible to spiritual attachment, given the right circumstances.

It's during these times that there may be areas of weakness in your energy. If you're feeling bad enough, your own Spirit may have checked out from your body momentarily, floating around, waiting to return at a time when you're feeling better.

When your guard is down is when Attachment Spirits can jump on board and tap into your energy or completely takeover.

Attachment Spirits exist wherever humans exist but do tend to congregate in areas where there's a lot of death. This is mostly because this is where they get "stuck" when trying to find a way to get energy with which to move around. Hospitals, near-death events, and last rite areas such as cemeteries are examples of areas with a density of Attachment Spirits.

How it Harms
Dealing with an Attachment Spirit is suddenly having to support the energetic requirements of two adults on the energy supply of one.
In a way, it's kind of like being pregnant. Except in pregnancy you're supporting the energy needs of yourself and of a tiny, growing baby that you know and love.

In the case of Attachments, you're supporting the energy of yourself, and at least one other individual who is likely a grown adult and of whom you know nothing.

They could be a perfectly nice person or they could also be a drug addict. It could be someone that died from an illness and because they haven't crossed over they have not healed. They are now transferring the symptoms of their illness to you as they attach.

Additionally, temperament can transfer from the attached spirit to their human host. A spirit harboring intense anger could pass the feelings of anger and resentment off and the host ends up and displaying the resulting behaviors.

It's like sharing your ice pop with a stranger, who could very well have a disease that will be passed to you through the sharing exchange.

When an Attachment Spirit connects themselves to you, there is an automatic exchange of energy. As the link is made, energy is re-routed primarily to the spirit then to your physical body secondarily.

This process can cause physical illness, behavioral changes, and emotional distress of varying degrees depending on the intensity of the Attachment.

Attachment Spirits can drastically change the behavior of those to whom they attach. Have you ever been in a relationship with someone, (be it a friendship or romantic relationship) who was angry, irritable, and mean and you noticed those traits rubbing off on you? It's the same concept.

You're sharing space, and in this case, energy, so you're sharing attitudes.

Only here, you likely don't even know the person or that it's happening in the first place. The main symptom of an Attachment Spirit is often fatigue, which is a symptom for so many other things, that most people don't even notice or know a Spirit could be causing the drain.

With this continual demand on your energy, you may feel lethargic, tired and exhausted always. The Attachment Spirit depletes your energy. They can also cause physical illness, and with a lack of energy for an immune response, you could get sicker than you would normally get on your own.

If the Attachment Spirit has chosen to attach themselves to a certain area of your body, your stomach for example, you can experience dysfunction in that area due to the energy re-rerouting and general disturbance to your system that an Attachment Spirit wreaks.

Attachment Spirits can cause and perpetuate addiction.

If you have recently developed an addiction or are struggling with an ongoing addiction, consider that it is not you at all but an Attachment Spirit who is manipulating your behavior for the sole purpose of living vicariously through the body of a living person.

This is real. It does happen and it happens often.

Addicts who die do not always cross over. And when they don't, they aren't healed of their addiction, like they would be if they went into the Light. Their earthly problems still exist and they will do anything to get more of whatever it is to which they were addicted. Now they're dead and don't have a body with which to partake in the activity and feel the results. Obviously the next viable option is to manipulate someone who is alive to their benefit. This can mean keeping someone an addict despite their intent to get clean, or it can mean turning a new person into an addict.

Attachment Spirits are often the force behind mental illness.

This is especially the case in bipolar disorder and personality disorders. Depending on the power of the Attachment Spirit and the vulnerability of the living person, the degree to which an Attachment Spirit can change the behavior and personality of the living can vary in severity to match the severity of mental illness. Drastic and sudden behavior and personality changes is often the work of an Attachment Spirit, a dead person or entity, who has taken over the body of the living in whole or in part.

These are just a few of the problems Attachment Spirits can cause, though the list is much longer.

Spirits who attach themselves to the living can and do cause a great amount of harm.

The good news is that Attachment Spirits do not have to be a lifelong curse should you have one attached. They aren't something you have to live with forever, or even that long, if you don't want to. (And who really does?) As soon as you recognize a problem, either a long-time illness, or a sudden behavioral or personality change, you have the option to a see a Shaman.

Shamans can help you get rid of Attachment Spirits. A Shaman is someone that heals the spiritual and the energetic body, and in doing so is able to release and remove any Spiritual Attachments that are causing problems.

Once you know about Spiritual Attachments and how it can happen, you can prevent it.

Having an Attachment Spirit is no one's fault. Everyone experiences periods of vulnerability throughout their lives and it is during these times that susceptibility to disease of any kind, may appear.

It is through these experiences, we learn, and sometimes that learning is what guides us to learning about the influence of the Spirit World, too.

CHAPTER 5: THE FOUR TYPES OF HAUNTINGS

TYPES OF HAUNTINGS

The word "haunting" has broad implications and we often use this word to encompass a wide spectrum of paranormal phenomena.

Haunting is not exclusive to the presence of a ghost or human spirit. A haunting could come at the hand of any numerous type of entity.

To better understand what we mean when we say haunting, we have broken this broad term down into four widely accepted types of haunting.

Residual Hauntings

Haunting, in this case, is a misnomer as it is not much of a haunting at all. Instead it is more like a recording of a specific energy or event destined to replay on a loop unaware that time has moved on.

It is a commonly held belief that a residual haunting is created when a person releases a massive amount of energy or experiences extreme heightened emotions of fear and anxiety within a room or space. This type of energy is an imprint or a lingering energy. Residual hauntings are the most common type of hauntings.

Residual hauntings do not involve a ghost or a spirit interacting with the living. The phantoms and events associated with this occurrence are unaware of the living. This type of haunting is a remnant of a long past traumatic event that happened at or near a location where a person has died traumatically and left their energy imprinted at that location.

Signs of a Residual Haunting:

The spirit does not seem to interact with or acknowledge the living. This type of spirit will be oblivious to anything that is occurring in the present moment.

There have been cases in which the apparitions come and go with only the sound of their footsteps heard by the living. Others report items moving around with no earthly explanation.

The energy felt in a residual haunting may have a tremendous impact on the individual experiencing this type of apparition. There is absolutely nothing to fear, this type of haunting cannot harm you in any way.

The energy from a residual haunting can interrupt electricity and electrical appliances. Security cameras have captured instances of doors opening and closing on their own. This is just energy, Nothing else. It is not a presence, there is no conscious effort on the behalf of this type of spirit when it comes to this certain type of activity. The ghost does not respond to you or to your questions or even acknowledge that you are there.

Some examples or a residual haunting are:

At 10:00 P.M. nightly, a ghostly apparition of a lady is seen at the upstairs window of the home.

At 8:00 P.M. every Wednesday you hear footsteps across the hallway.

These instances are indicative of a routine or event that has been imprinted into our physical world and plays on a loop without regard to the living occupying the space.

Intelligent Haunting

If a residual haunting is defined as an event that occurs without regard to or acknowledgment from the living, then an intelligent haunting is the exact opposite.

An intelligent haunting event usually occurs when the spirits are aware of and can communicate with the living, and desire the attention from the living. Their abilities include but are not limited to moving or hiding objects, sending signs, and knocking pictures off the walls.

The reasons for intelligent hauntings range from the desire to connect with loved ones and the living in general to passing on a message and taking care of unfinished business. Intelligent hauntings usually occur during the late-night hours. Very rarely does this type of paranormal activity transpire during the day, this is due to gathering up energy resources. Intelligent hauntings are perpetrated by spirits usually who died suddenly.

As a result, they are unaware that they are dead and they will stick around for their family and friends or due to an attachment to a location or a home.

Signs to look for in the area or areas of an intelligent hauntings are: cold spot, experiencing unnatural causes of chills and goosebumps, or a feeling that someone is staring at you or standing behind you.

These are spirits who refuses to move on because of unfinished business or in some cases are afraid to be judged and sent to hell. These types of spirits are not evil or malicious. They just want to be heard. It is best to have a voice recorder to record their messages.

After all, that is what the spirit is after, being heard or acknowledged.

Intelligent hauntings are not like residual hauntings. Intelligent hauntings have complete consciousness and are aware of you and their surroundings. These types of Spirits have been known to interact with the living.

There are many possibilities and reasons why that this type of spirit stays on our physical plane.

1. Many spirits that are Intelligent simply may not know or realized that they are dead and they are still trying to continue living as before prior to their death. This is very common among people who had a sudden or very quick death. Their conscious did not process that they are dying or had died or they did not experience a consciousness of death.

2. Some spirits stay behind due to their free will to try to continue to protect their loved ones and Friends.

3. There might be an attachment or connection to place, items, or a person on this physical plane.

4. Many and very common that these types of spirits feel that is their obligation to send a very important message to a loved one.

5. In some cases, it may be associated with their fear of death and that they are frightened to move on from life to death or that they need more time to get used to the fact that they are dead. Most common one is the Religion type. They fear of going to hell. It is possible in this spirit's life prior to death that they believed that they sinned too much or made too many mistakes to go to Heaven for their fear of

judgment and being sent to hell for an eternity or a similar hellish residence.

When it comes to intelligent hauntings, my observations are that there is a consciousness behind these types of spirits and they have their personality intact.

For example, if they were angry in life they will be angry spirits. Never confuse an angry spirit with a demonic one which has never been human in the first place. Conversely, an intelligent spirit that was kind in life will be kind in the afterlife.

Signs of Intelligent Hauntings
1. You may feel as if there is someone present that you cannot see.
2. You will feel ominous or creepy.
3. Cold chills.
4. A general feeling of unease.
5. You may see an apparition.
6. You may see lights go on and off by itself.
7. Radios turn on by themselves.
8. Floating objects by unseen hands.
9. Unusual sounds like chirps, grunting clearing of a voice.
10. A voice that speaks to you.
11. A light touch on body like a brush of a hand that isn't there on the shoulder.
12. Signs like birds or coincidences associated with you and your loved one.

Poltergeist Hauntings

The word poltergeist is a German word for noisy ghost. The German word "Polter" which means to make noises and "Geist", meaning ghost or spirit.

Poltergeist hauntings typically involve objects being moved, hidden, or thrown across the rooms.

Disturbing noises such as loud ringing, high pitch sounds like chirping, and shouting are known to accompany a poltergeist haunting. Poltergeists also interfere with electronic devices such as television, radios, computers, laptops, and cellphones.

A poltergeist can physically attack people and are thought to be linked to spontaneous human combustion, a very rare phenomenon in and of itself.

Poltergeists are known for making objects quickly disappear and reappear. There is some belief that poltergeist activity is created by subconscious psycho/telekinesis of troubled individuals who may be unaware of their latent psychic abilities.

Poltergeist hauntings have been associated with young teenage girls or boys who are under extreme stress or trauma.

Poltergeists can be either playful or malicious and because of the nature of the haunting are often mistaken for demonic activity.

This type of haunting usually starts slow with what is commonly referred to as the "infestation period" where the entity slowly makes its presence known, starting with scratching sounds and knocking.

Over time the activity increases until it reaches to its peak. It is at the peak of activity that a poltergeist is most dangerous and may set small fires.

Eventually the phenomenon ceases.

There has not been a known case of repeated poltergeist activity due to exhaustion of all the spirit's energy. A case of repetitive poltergeist activity could be indicative of a greater threat, such as a demonic presence.

Signs of Poltergeist Hauntings

You may notice that things often don't appear to be right where you left them, instead the items are in a unusual location or you cannot find them at all.

1. You smell four odors. Rotting meat, sewage- but check if you have a dead mouse somewhere or a sewage leak. It could also be a sign of a demonic spirit. (Demonic hauntings also have foul odors.)

2. Levitating objects- such as knives. Take precaution!

3. Broken objects suddenly begin working again. Grandfather clocks, desk clocks, televisions, radios, toys without batteries in them (or the batteries are dead.)

4. You are being attacked by something that isn't there. Poltergeist are notorious for hurting people. You may wake up to bruises in strange areas of your body and you can't determine a logical reason for their appearance. You may also have hand or fingerprint shaped bruises on your body as if someone has grabbed you forcefully. You may

experience the following by an unseen force: slapping, dragging, hitting, pinching, pushing, hair pulling, and tripping.

5. Your Dog is suddenly afraid to come in the house. Pets can sense things even when we can't. A family pet refusing to enter the house or a room is a sign that there could be a poltergeist present. Pay attention to animal behaviors such as your dog or cat becoming obsessed with a certain spot in the room.

6. Your child starts talking to inanimate objects. Ghosts and Poltergeists like to pretend they are something else like a benevolent spirit. If your child is suddenly speaking to the television when the television is off or if they are having conversations with their toys or other inanimate objects, you might be experiencing a poltergeist. It is important to note that these behaviors must be out of character for your child, as in a sudden change in behaviors and activity.

Common Objects of Poltergeist interest are:

- Children toys
- Plates
- Glasses
- Dishware
- Small objects such as ceramic decorations
- Dog toys
- Balls
- Stuffed toy animals or dolls
- Shampoo bottles
- Wall decorations

Regular blessings usually do not work in cases like Poltergeist Hauntings. Historically, poltergeist cases must run their course before there is a return to normalcy.

Demonic Hauntings

In demonic hauntings, the intent is to break down a person's free will so that the entity can take over and fully possess the individual that the demon had targeted.

The demonic is a deceptive spirit that enters a home or an area to cause harm and to destroy all that is good.

The demon not only possesses people, it can attach itself to an object of their choosing. Common objects are: Dolls, Rings, Paintings and sometimes clothes.

They start out as a benevolent spirit, seemingly serving only to help to people. They can also mimic poltergeist hauntings with small disturbances such as knocking on walls, objects being moved, doors closing and opening on their own.

The most common sights are that the demon may appear as a black, very dark shadow. It will initially appear as a benevolent or helpful spirit only. When the demon is found out, it reveals itself.

Foul odors, extreme temperatures changes, and even physical attacks such as scratches begin occurring. Attacks usually transpire in threes, to mock the Trinity (The Father, The Son and The Holy Spirit.)

Demons have the ability to shapeshift from human to an animal form. The demon will try to convince the victim that it is no longer there. The demon is being dormant until it is time for an attack.

The demon becomes stronger when it senses fear and at times when the victims are usually weak, vulnerable, or ill.

As the demon becomes stronger it will strike, escalating to a full possession.

This type of Haunting needs an exorcism by a priest only. Seek guidance from paranormal investigators, clergymen, and others who are extremely familiar with demonic hauntings.

This Haunting is the most dangerous one of all. Protect yourself and family. Most of all don't wait too long! Call a professional that specializes in these types of hauntings.

Most paranormal investigators agree that cases involving a demon are rare. There are a handful signs to look for in demonic hauntings.

1. Banging noises
2. Low growls
3. Foul smells, such as urine or rotten meat. The most definite sign of a demonic haunting is the inexplicable presence of sulfuric odor.
4. The air will feel heavy or oppressive. The most common affected areas in the home are the attic, basement, and bedrooms.
5. Emotionally affected, the victim will experience extreme emotions such as: fear, anxiety and anger.
6. Sleep disturbances. The victim will suffer from sleep complications. This is due to that most demonic hauntings are more active during the night. The Peak time for these occurs are well known around three to three thirty in the mornings. Even though the victim has spent enough time resting, they often awake feeling as if they have haven't rested at all.
7. One of the top signs of a demonic haunting is when a pet such as a dog or a cat act erratically. Examples of erratic behavior in pets include but are not limited to; withdraw from family members, aggression, fear of certain rooms within the house,

growling or barking at unseen things, and running in fear from unseen forces.
8. Victims will start to lose interest in things that they once loved. They may start missing school or work or withdraw from family and friends. They are most likely being oppressed or being Possessed by a demon.
9. Children begin to see things in their bedrooms such as a shadow or will claim that a nice man or woman comes to them in their bedrooms at night. The apparition will at first seem very kind and unthreatening, then turn suddenly. Children will wake up in the middle of the night screaming and claim that someone is hurting them.
10. Adults will wake up with unexplained scratches on their body.
11. Very high EMF readings are present throughout the house or building with no mechanical explanation
12. Feeling someone or something else is controlling you.
13. Feeling like someone or something is pressuring you to do certain acts that you do not particular want to do.
14. Hearing one or multiple voices in your head that are negative, persuasive or commanding.
15. Deep personality changes
16. Creepy feelings.
17. Feeling cold all the time or hot.
18. An area of your house or in the neighborhood that feels oppressive or negative.
19. An aversion to prayers or an inability to pray.
20. Shadows in your peripheral vision.
21. Flickering lights and electronics.
22. Hearing faint screams
23. An increase of arguments and fights in home.

The most succinct sign of a demonic presence is the overall feeling of oppression and negativity. A demon strives to drive a wedge between family and sow discord. It thrives on the negative energy and hostile environment.

CHAPTER 6: DEMONOLOGY-KNOW YOUR ENEMY

THE DEMON DICTIONARY A TO Z

The following list of demons and the subsequent descriptions of each is meant as a primer, as such this list is not all-inclusive. The full book of demons is lengthy and encompasses demons present in all religions.

It is believed that if you know the name of the demon then it can be cast out. Our goal here is to provide a high-level resource, but you are encouraged to seek out more robust works such as "Names of the Damned-The Dictionary of Demons" by Michelle Belanger or visit www.demonicpedia.com

Abbacus
This demon is associated with the Ouija Board.

Abaddon
The book of Revelation says that Abaddon is described as the king of locusts and is the angel of the abyss of hell. In the scriptures Abaddon is actually referred to the place of utter destruction and he is called the "chief of the demons" and also is referred as the angel of death. Signs to look for are: Locust, Flies and unnatural deaths such as birds or other small animals in the same location with no explanation to why that is. Also known by the Greek name *Apollyon*.

Abezi-Thibod
A red-winged demon that is involved with dark magic. One of the damned prices of Egypt who became a demon of the sea upon the drowning of Pharaoh's army. Also, the son of Beelzebub.

Abraxas
A demon associated with magic and is the source of the common name Abracadabra.

Abyzou
A female demon that is associated with miscarriages and infant mortality.

Aeshma
A demon associated with wrath, rage, and fury.

Agrat bat Mahlat
A demon associated with magic and illness resulted from using magic on oneself or on another.

Agares
A demon associated with earthquakes and teaches the languages of immoral expression.

Ahab
A demon associated with giving up on authority and responsibility.

Ahriman
A demon associated with deceptive evil thinking and thoughts.

Aim
A demon associated with manipulation and is a familiar spirit.

Ala
A demon associated with bad weather and strong winds and is shown as a female.

Alal
A demon associated with sexual demon. The description is of a female demon with dark hair, large eyes and a round-like face.

Alaster
A demon associated with possession brought on by a curse.

Alloces
A demon associated with immorality and astrology and tries to induce the desire for divination and mysticism. Known as The Great Duke of Hell who appears in the shape of a knight riding a winged horse. Also known as *Allocer*.

Alû
A demon associated with spirit possession that will result in unconsciousness and coma. This demon has no mouth, lips or ears. The demon will roam at night and try to terrify people while they are sleeping.

Amy
This demon is a male figure and will appear as fire before taking the shape of man. He is a demon of astrology and liberal sciences.

Andras
A demon who sows discord among people. Seen as a winged angel with a head of an owl or a raven.

Andrealphus
This demon is described as a peacock. It is associated with astrology and geometry and can turn man into a bird!

Andromalius
This demon can gain information about any objects or people and locations. He appears as a man holding a great serpent.

Anzu
This demon is associated with psychics and predicting the future and appears as a large bird or vulture.

Asag
This a monstrous looking demon, whose appearance is said to cause fish to boil in the river, can shapeshift into any animal to instill fear into any man.

Asakku
This demon attacks and kills man by the means of fever. This demon can induce fevers in people.

Asclepeion
A demon associated with false healing.

Asmodai
A demon associated with twisting people's desires, wants and needs.

Baalor or Bael
A demon associated with sky and the land of farming and can appear as a bearded older man with curling ram's horns.

Balberith
A demon associated with tempting man to blasphemy and murder.

Banshee
A demon associated with a female spirit as an omen of death and can be heard as a loud screeching owl or monkey.

Carabia
This demon is shown as a pentagram star, changing into a man under the summing request.

Choronzon
This demon function is to destroy the ego.

Cimejes
This demon warrior can locate lost or hidden treasures and has the teaching ability such as grammar, logic and rhetoric.

Crocellor or Procell
A demon associated with the tendency to speak in a dark and very dark mysterious sayings and riddles.

Culsa
A demon associated with gateways and deaths. This demon appears as a topless winged woman carrying a lit torch and scissors.

Dajjal
This demon is associated with the appearance of the messiah or pretending to be the Messiah.

Dantalion
This demon is associated with the Arts and Science, and claims to know the thoughts of all people and can change them at his will. This demon has the abilities to cause love and to cause an wish fulfillment vision.

Decarabia
This demon is associated with herbs and precious stones and can transform into any type of bird and can act like a familiar spirit.

Drekavac
This demon is associated with screaming. The appearance is like a dog or a fox and has hind legs similar to a kangaroo.

Eldonna
This demon is associated with the demons of Incubus and Succubus. This demon is a perverted sexual demon.

Eligor
This demon is associated with hidden things and knows the future of wars and how the soldiers will meet.

Eisheth
This demon is associated with the woman of whoredom.

Eblis
This demon is associated with Infirmity.

Focalor
This demon is associated with killing men in ships by overthrowing Warships.

Foras
This demon is associated with teaching of all herbs and precious stones and tries to make men witty, invisible and to live a long time.

Furfur
This demon is associated with lying and to cause love between two partners usually with adultery.

Gaap
This demon is associated with the powers to teach philosophy and can make people invisible and can render a man into stupidity.

Gader'el
This Fallen angel is associated with cosmetics and weapons. This Angel can teach people on new tech cosmetics and weapons of war.

Glasya-Labolas
This demon is associated with manslaughter, science and can cause love among others if desired and can incite homicides and can make a person invisible.

Gorgon
This demon is associated with the ability to turn anyone into stone if looked at the snakes in its hair like Medusa.

Gremory
This demon is associated with the things of the past, present and the future. This demon has the appearance of a beautiful woman riding on a camel.

Gualichu
This demon is associated with possession of men to its liking.

Guayota
This demon is associated with an appearance of a black dog that was accompanied by other demon black dogs.

Gusion
A strong Great Duke of Hell, and rules over forty legions of demons. He tells all past, present and future things, shows the meaning of all questions that are asked to him, reconciles friends, and gives honor and dignity.
This demon is associated with an appearance of a baboon.

Hat Man
A demon associated with an appearance of a black shadow wearing a top hat or fedora. This demon is associated with dark Arts and the Ouija boards.

Halphas
A demon associated with an appearance of a stork and can start wars.

Incubus
A demon associated with the appearance of a male, now to seduce women at night This demon abilities are for causing overwhelming sexual urges in the body, his demon is responsible for sexual dreams and overall lascivious behavior.

Ipos
A demon associated with wit and valor (sometimes false.) is an Earl of hell who commands thirty-six lesser demons. He appears with the head of a lion and has the tail of a hare and webbed feet of a goose.

Ishtar
A demon from Middle Eastern lore associated with fertility, love, sex and war; displays cruelty toward men. Thought to be the personification of the planet Venus.

Irritum
A demon associated with "Nothingness" This demon is a spirit of depression, worthlessness and despair.

Jezebel
This demon type is associated with false prophets and lust and sometimes greed. It should be noted that Jezebel is a spirit type and not the proper name of the demon. Many demons can be Jezebel Spirits, so you must research the particular spirit to derive the proper name.

Jikininki
A Japanese demon is associated with corpses- eating spirits or devouring the flesh of the corpses.

Kasadya
This fallen Angel is associated with murder, abortion and can destroy the fetus within the uterus. Also, the demon of snake bites and sunstroke. Responsible for teaching mankind herbology and how to perform abortions.

Labal
A small black demon with demonic energy flowing from his eyes This demon is associated with vampirism and the draining of human energy and spirit.

Lechies
This Russian demon is associated with the woods and thrive there. It appears with a lower humanoid half with the upper torso taking on the form of a horned goat. They are associated with kidnapping young women from the woods.

Leyak
Demon from Indonesian folklore who takes on the form of a floating head, said to fly around seeking pregnant women from which to suck the unborn's blood.

Lempo
This demon is associated with being an erratic spirit and can cause destructiveness in those she possesses.

Leviathan
Portrayed as sea serpent, this demon is associated with the spiritual pride

Louts
A demon associated with uncouth and aggressive behavior. Profane and confrontational.

Lilith
A female demon associated disease, illness, death, wind, and storms. Appears as a night bird or screech-owl.

Maricha
A demon associated with kidnapping and the ability to shapeshift into animals.

Moloch
A demon associated with idolatry and child sacrificing. Also known as Molech, Milcom, or Malcam

Naamah
A demon who is the mate of the archangel Samael and is the mother of the plagues of mankind. The demon is known for her ability to cause epilepsy in children.

Naberius
A demon associated with the appearance of a three-headed dog or a raven. A Great Marquis of Hell with a notable hoarse voice who restores lost dignities and teaches men the art of gracious living.

Namtar
Hellish minor deity in Mesopotamian folklore. Responsible for disease and death. Is said to command sixty diseases in the form of demons that can penetrate different parts of the human body.

Orias
A demon associated with the knowledge of the stars and planets.

Orishas
This fallen Angel is a troublesome one and is associated with the Constellation Aquarius. He enjoys strangling people who are born under the sign of the Aquarius. This fallen angel's abilities include the gift of prophecy, shape shifting, and causing physical pain with merely a touch.
 The appearance of this angel is usually a lion or a heavenly creature with wings. This Angel is associated with falling stars. These demons fly towards heaven to overhear God's plans and they fall back to Earth, appearing as a shooting star to the naked human eye.

Paimon
This demon is associated with familiar spirits and binding men to familiars to do their deed. Has knowledge of past and future events, can create visions and hallucinations, and is known to reanimate the dead for several years. Appears as a man riding a crowned camel.

Petula
A demon associated with the addiction of games and general antisocial behavior.

Pruflas
A Great Prince and Duke of Hell, this demon is associated with making men to commit discord, quarrels, and falsehoods. This demon should not be granted admission to any place, but if conjured will provide truthful answer to inquiries.

Python
A demon associated with divinations and dark arts or magic. The appearance is a python snake that tightens its hold on victims. Empowers fortune tellers and tarot readers.

Rah
This demon is associated with worshipping the Sun. Idols.

Rahab
A demon from Jewish folklore who represents the demonic angel of the sea. A representation of the primordial abyss, darkness and chaos.

Raum
A demon associated with kidnapping. The abilities are to shapeshift into a large crow. One of the Great Earls of Hell ruling thirty legions of demons. He is the destroyer of cities and the dignities of man. Knower of all things past, present, and future. *Also known as R'am or Raim*

Raul or Roul
A demon associated with lasciviousness, sexual corruption, and overseer of houses of ill repute.

Ronove
A demon associated with near death of human and animals. The demon appears as a monster cloaked in a black robe and holding a staff. This demon is described as a taker of old souls.

Rusalka
This demon is associated with water, it is described as a water nymph, a female spirit.

Rakshasa
Bengali/Hindi female shape shifting demon, considered a man-eater with flaming red hair and eyes and long razor-sharp talons. Desires human blood and flesh.

Ravan
A ten-headed Hindi demon associated with magic, idolatry, and divination.

Sabnock
This demon is associated with war. The appearance is of a soldier with armor and weapons with a head of a lion and is seen riding a pale horse. The abilities are to create war and injuries.

Samael
This fallen archangel is associated with death or is known as the Demon of death. He is an accuser, seducer, and destroyer.

Samurai
These demons prevalent in Japanese folklore and culture are associated with seeking to restructure the entire world to their desires.

Scox
This demon is associated with taking away sight, hearing and the understanding of people. This demon endorses people to look down on the deaf, blind, and the mentally handicap, His appearance is of a stork that has a hoarse but a subtle voice.

Shadow Person
This demon is associated with fear. He feeds off fear and anxiety usually goes away when the victim is calmed down and is thinking good, positive thoughts. Positive energy flow from within a person is repellant against shadow people.

Sitri
This demon is associated with a strong, complete control over relationships, chaos, and the darkness. Sitri is known for the murder of individuals who stand in its way.

Stenno
A demon associated with murder. The appearance is monstrous in nature with the demon brandishing brass hands and sharp fangs. Its hair is formed of living venomous snakes.

Succubus
A vampiric dream-demon who takes on the appearance of a woman to seduce men through sexual activity. Through sexual interaction with male hosts, the demon drains the energy force of the living and can bend the host to her desires. Can sow discord and hostility within families and communities.

Tommyknocker
This demon is associated with poltergeist but, is found in Tombs and caverns rather than in regular homes.

Ukobach
A lesser demon with red or fiery skin who carries a pan of hot coals or a red-hot poker and are tasked with stoking the fires of hell.

Uvall
This demon is associated with the love of women. The appearance is of a man who speaks the Egyptian language imperfectly. This demon has a deep voice and the abilities are that this demon can make men friends with their foes.

Valac
This demon is associated with giving true answers about hidden treasures. The appearance of this demon is a small boy with angel wings.

Vine
This demon is associated with bringing down walls, buildings, and towers. The appearance of this demon is as a lion holding a snake in his hand and riding a black horse.

Wendigo
This demon is associated with cannibalism. The ability of this demon is to be able to shapeshift into a person.

Xezbeth

This demon is associated with lies and rumors and legends. The abilities of this demon is to invent untrue tales. It is a manipulator and can pretend to be other demons by its disingenuous nature. The arabic name of this demon, Al-Kathab, literally means "The Liar".

Zozo or Zaza

This demon is associated with the Ouija board and is predatory in nature. It is commonly thought of as a male spirit due to its perverse obsession with women. This demon is known to prey on those who are weak, depressed, and suicidal. It can infect the mind of a Ouija user and slowly drive them to madness; the effect can take years to manifest. This demon is also known as Pazuzu, made famous by the novel "The Exorcist".

CHAPTER 7: EXORCISM-EXPEL ALL EVIL AWAY FROM YOU

The belief in evil and the belief that evil can be cast out is the basis for the ritual known as "exorcism", whereby attachment spirits and demons are expelled from a living host.

The Three Stages of Demonic Possession
1) The first stage is **manifestation and infestation**. This can occur in homes, buildings, cars and even inanimate objects like toys and dolls.

Demons typically come in a form of something you would trust, such as a little girl or a loved one. This demon is seeking approval at this stage to be invited and to stay.

Signs of infestation are:

- Smells of sulfur, feces and urine is associated with foul spirits.
- Groups of three knocks or banging sounds
- Physical- Being pushed, bitten and even dragged around.
- Religious items being broken or disappeared.
- Mood swings so severe that medical help is needed and there is no explanation for this.
- Disembodied voices
- Feelings of depression

2) The second stage- **Oppression**

This stage is where the demonic entity makes itself known and moves into full attack mode. The demon will attack and exhaust the mental and physical facilities of its victim, affecting their overall will to live.

The demon will accomplish this through sleep deprivation, a heightened paranormal activity, physical assault (scratches, bites, and burns) and sexual assault.

The most common form of oppression is wrought through the resulting depression of the victim. Depression affects the will and faith of the victim to a breaking point, ultimately resulting in surrender to the demon.

Signs of Oppression are:

- Victim was outgoing or liked to go out to do things but, now they isolate themselves
- Mood swings, Anger, outbursts of Wrath.
- Hearing voices
- Sees things that are not there.
- Markings on the body such as scratches, bruising etc.
- Zoning out a lot and then it turns into trances like states for longer periods of time.
- Psychic abilities- Like knowing things that they wouldn't know otherwise

3) The third stage- **Possession**

This the most dangerous of all stages. Possession now has the victim in its grasp. At this stage, the victim will have little to no self- worth or faith, their will is almost completely gone.

Signs of Possession are:

- The possessed hear voices telling them to inflict emotional and physical pain on others.
- The demon now can control the body like a parasite.
- The victim may speak in a foreign language of which they are unfamiliar
- Displays of superhuman strength
- Ability to move objects without touching them (Telekinesis)
- Self-injurious behaviors (Cutting, biting, or burning)
- Ingestion of vile items such as bodily fluids and waste, or insects and vermin, etc...
- Urinating or defecating themselves
- Saying the most hurtful things that a human would not say to another

An exorcism must be performed by a priest or ordained minister. Performing an exorcism is dangerous and there are many risks and dangers involved in dealing with demonic forces.

An exorcism will not work if you are afraid. You must not fear the evil spirits/demons. Fear is their food, they feed on our fear (and negative emotions). You must not be sad or depressed. You must not be full of anger. You must be full of love and light. They cannot stand love and light.

You most likely will not be able to cast out an evil spirit from another person's body or another person's home. If somebody has invited an evil spirit into their body or home either consciously or subconsciously, then only that person can rescind the invitation and cast the evil spirit out.

People may have moved into a home that has been previously possessed by evil spirits or malevolent ghosts at the invite of a prior resident.

It is possible that a person can inadvertently invite an evil spirit into their body through the committing of "sin" (evil deeds), or doing drugs and alcohol. Demons also attack the weak, innocent, and helpless.

Mental disorders will open you up to let the demons possess you as well. I personally believe that people who hear voices are under demonic attack and on the way to full-blown demonic possession.

A lot of people are partially possessed and don't even know it. Partial possession is when the demon inhabits a part of a host body and causes the host physical and emotional problems. At this point the demon or spirit does not have full control over the host's mind, body, and soul.
In a full possession, the soul becomes completely overwhelmed and the demonic force does more severe physical, emotional and psychological damage.

Demonic possessions are classified on three levels: mild, medium, and severe.

Mild possession is indicated by such behaviors as aggression from a normally docile person, hysterical laughter, and talking gibberish etc. An average person of a moderate spiritual level can speak to the person and calm them down.

Medium levels of possession are indicated by the same set of occurrences as a mild possession but includes a heightened sixth sense or extra sensory perception. The symptoms are far more pronounced than the mild possession. A spiritually average person is limited in their ability to calm the afflicted.

Severe possession symptoms include all the trademarks of mild and medium level possessions but also include profane language, physical harm to self and others, and the disappearance of the host's mental identity completely.
 This type of possession can only be diagnosed by a saint of the highest order. A spiritually average person cannot calm them down.

Exorcism is not, and has never been, limited to Christianity. Shamans from all ancient cultures have helped people (or attempted to help people) rid or cleanse themselves of evil spirits from a lower vibration/realm.

Depending on the spiritual beliefs of the exorcist, exorcism may be done by causing the entity to swear an oath of departure or by performing an elaborate ritual, or simply by commanding the entity to depart the host in the name of a higher power.

The act of exorcism involves continual repetition of prayers, removal orders, and the use of objects that can repel the entity. Such relics include but are not limited to crucifixes, holy water, rosaries, and ceremonial beads and shakers.

Here are some signs of demonic invasion:

- Cutting, scratching, and biting of the skin
- Cold feeling in the room
- Unnatural bodily postures and contortions
- Losing control of their normal personality and entering a frenzy or rage and or attacking others
- Change in the host's voice

- Supernatural strength
- Speaking in a foreign language with which they are unfamiliar and untrained
- Violent reactions toward all religious objects or items
- Antipathy towards entering a church, speaking Jesus' name, or hearing scriptures.

Rules for Exorcism

An exorcism must be done by a priest with proper authorization and knowledge of how to perform the rite.

More than one person should be present preferably family members.

Incorporate the use of The Saint Benedict Medal into the ceremony. It is a sacramental medal containing symbols and texts related to the life of Saint Benedict of Nursia. It's the oldest and most honored medal used by Catholics, and due to the belief in its power against evil it is also known as the "devil-chasing medal".

Prayers to be used in conjunction with the medal are:

- Prayer to All Angels
- Prayer to St. Michael the Archangel
- Angel of my Save
- Prayer to the Archangel Uriel
- Under Your Protection
- The Lord's Prayer
- Hail Mary
- Prayer to love God

These prayers are found under the protection chapter.

There are some other things that will keep the malevolent spirits from coming back but please keep in mind that without telling the spirit(s) to leave, these things will not work.

After you have cast out the evil spirit, here is what you can do to keep them from coming back:

- Clean up your act. Cleanliness is next to godliness
- Keep your body clean
- Keep your house clean.
- Let lots of light (and fresh air) into your home.
- Go outside and get plenty of sunlight. (Evil spirits absolutely abhor sunlight
- Think positive thoughts, evil spirits cannot abide positivity
- Love. Find opportunities to love others. Service is nice way to express your love for others.
- Create a pleasant environment in your home. Use incense or scented candles. Also, add some wholesome and uplifting art to your home.
- Most Importantly, you must forgive! Forgive everyone that has ever hurt you. Holding grudges lowers your vibrations.
- Moderation in all things. Resist the temptation to indulge in vices, especially drugs. Drugs (including too much alcohol) can lower your resistance to evil spirits
- Find a cause. Fight for what is right
- Never fear. Fear is a lower vibration. If you know the truth, and if you are prepared, ye shall not fear.
- Invite your guardian angels to surround you with their light, love and support.

An Exorcism Prayer (To be said by a Priest only)

This is a prayer against Satan and his rebellious angels. It was published by the Order of His Holiness Pope Leo XIII.

The term "exorcism" does NOT always denote a solemn exorcism involving a person possessed by the devil. In general, the term denotes prayers to "curb the power of the devil and prevent him from doing harm." As St. Peter had written in Holy Scripture, "your adversary the devil, as a roaring lion, goes about seeking whom he may devour." [1 St.Peter. 5:8]

The Holy Father exhorts priests to say this prayer as often as possible, as a simple exorcism to curb the power of the devil and prevent him from doing harm. The faithful also may say it in their own name, for the same purpose, as any approved prayer. Its use is recommended whenever action of the devil is suspected, causing malice in men, violent temptations and even storms and various calamities. It could be used as a solemn exorcism (an official and public ceremony, in Latin), to expel the devil. It would then be said by a priest, in the name of the Church and only with a Bishop's permission.

Prayer to St. Michael the Archangel
In the Name of the Father,
and of the Son,
and of the Holy Ghost.
Amen.

Most glorious Prince of the Heavenly Armies,
Saint Michael the Archangel,
defend us in "our battle against principalities and
powers, against the rulers of this world of darkness,
against the spirits of wickedness in the high places"

[Eph., 6:12].

Come to the assistance of men whom God has created to His
likeness and whom He has redeemed at a great price from the tyranny
of the devil.

The Holy Church venerates you as her guardian and
protector; to you, the Lord has entrusted the souls of the redeemed
to be led into heaven. Pray therefore the God of Peace to
crush Satan beneath our feet, that he may no longer retain
men captive and do injury to the Church.

Offer our prayers to the Most High, that without delay they
may draw His mercy down upon us; take hold of "the
dragon, the old serpent, which is the devil and Satan," bind
him and cast him into the bottomless pit
"that he may no longer seduce the nations." [Rev. 20:2-3]

Exorcism

In the Name of Jesus Christ, our God and
Lord, strengthened by the intercession of the Immaculate
Virgin Mary, Mother of God,
of Blessed Michael the Archangel, of the
Blessed Apostles Peter and Paul and all the Saints, and
powerful in the holy authority of our ministry,
we confidently undertake to repulse the attacks and deceits
of the devil.

God arises; His enemies are scattered, and those who hate
Him flee before Him.

As smoke is driven away, so are they driven; as wax melts before the fire,
so the wicked perish at the presence of God.

V. Behold the Cross of the Lord, flee bands of enemies.
R. The Lion of the tribe of Juda, the offspring of David, hath conquered.

V. May Thy mercy, Lord, descend upon us.
R. As great as our hope in Thee.

We drive you from us, whoever you may be, unclean spirits, all satanic powers, all infernal invaders, all wicked legions, assemblies and sects.

In the Name and by the power of Our Lord Jesus Christ, may you be snatched away and driven from the Church of God and from the souls made to the image and likeness of God and redeemed by the **Precious Blood** of the Divine Lamb.

Most cunning serpent, you shall no more dare to deceive humans, persecute the Church, torment God's elect and sift them as wheat.

The Most High God commands you, He with whom, in your great insolence, you still claim to be equal.

"God who wants all men to be saved and to come to the knowledge of the truth." [1 Tim. 2:4)

God the Father commands you. God the Son commands you. God the Holy Ghost commands you.

Christ, God's Word made flesh, commands you; He who to save our race outdone through your envy, "humbled

Himself, becoming obedient even unto death" [Phil. 2:8]; He who has built His Church on the firm rock and declared that the gates of **hell** shall not prevail against Her, because He **will** dwell with Her "all days even to the end of the world." [Mt. 28:20]

The sacred Sign of the Cross commands you, as does also the power of the mysteries of the **Christian** Faith.

The glorious Mother of God, the Virgin Mary, commands you; she who by her **humility** and from the first moment of her **Immaculate Conception** crushed your proud head.

The **faith** of the holy **Apostles** Peter and Paul, and of the other **Apostles** commands you.

The blood of the Martyrs and the pious **intercession** of all the Saints command you.

Thus, cursed dragon, and you, diabolical legions, we adjure you by the living God, by the true God, by the holy God, by the **God** "who so loved the world that He gave up His Only Son, that every **soul** believing in Him might not perish but have **life** everlasting;" [St.Jn. 3:16] stop deceiving human creatures and pouring out to them the poison of eternal damnation; stop harming the Church and hindering her liberty.

Begone, Satan, inventor and master of all deceit, enemy of man's salvation.

Give place to **Christ** in Whom you have found **none** of your works; give place to the One, Holy, **Catholic** and Apostolic Church acquired by **Christ** at the price of His Blood.

Stoop beneath the all-powerful Hand of God; tremble and

flee when we invoke the Holy and terrible Name of Jesus, this Name which causes **hell** to tremble, this Name to which the Virtues, Powers and Dominations of **heaven** are humbly submissive, this Name which
the **Cherubim** and **Seraphim** praise unceasingly repeating: Holy, Holy, Holy is the Lord, the **God** of Hosts.

V. O Lord, hear my prayer.
R. And let my cry come unto Thee.

V. May the **Lord** be with thee.
R. And with thy spirit.

Let us pray.

God of heaven, God of earth, God of Angels, God of Archangels, God of Patriarchs, God of Prophets, God of Apostles, God of Martyrs, God of Confessors, God of Virgins, God who has power to give **life** after death and rest after work: because there is no other **God** than Thee and there can be no other, for Thou art the Creator of all things, visible and invisible, of Whose reign there shall be no end, we humbly prostrate ourselves before Thy glorious Majesty and we beseech Thee to deliver us by Thy
power from all the tyranny of the infernal spirits, from their snares, their lies, and their furious wickedness.

Deign, O Lord, to grant us Thy powerful protection and to keep us safe and sound. We beseech Thee through **Jesus Christ** Our Lord.

Amen.

V. From the snares of the devil,
R. Deliver us, O Lord.
V. That Thy Church may serve Thee in peace and liberty:

R. We beseech Thee to hear us.
V. That Thou may crush down all enemies of Thy Church:
R. We beseech Thee to hear us.

(Holy water is sprinkled in the place where we may be.)

The Act and Rite of Exorcism

The pastor delegated by the council to perform this rite should first go to confession, or at least elicit an act of contrition, and, if convenient, take the Lord's Supper and implore God's help in other fervent prayers.

He dresses just as he would on Sunday morning.

Having before him the person possessed (who should be bound if there is any danger), he traces the sign of the cross over the possessed, over himself, and over the bystanders before sprinkling them all with holy water.

He kneels and says the Lord's Prayer, exclusive of the prayers which follow it. All present are to make the responses. At the end of the prayer he adds the following:

Antiphon: Do not keep in mind, O Lord, our offenses or those of our parents, nor take vengeance on our sins.

The Lord's Prayer a second time (the rest inaudibly until:)

P: And lead us not into temptation.

All: But deliver us from evil.

Psalm 53

After the psalm, the pastor continues:

P: Save your servant.

All: Who trusts in you, my God.

P: Let him (her) find in you, Lord, a fortified tower.

All: In the face of the enemy.

P: Let the enemy have no power over him (her).

All: And the son of iniquity be powerless to harm him (her). Lord, send him (her) aid from your holy place.

All: And watch over him (her) from Heaven.

P: Lord, hear my prayer.

All: And let my cry be heard by you.

P: The Lord be with you.

All: May He also be with you.

P: Let us pray. God, whose nature is ever merciful and forgiving, accept our prayer that this servant of yours, bound by the fetters of sin, may be pardoned by your loving kindness. Holy Lord, almighty Father, everlasting God and Father of our Lord Jesus Christ, who once and for all consigned that fallen and apostate tyrant to the flames of Hell, who sent your only-begotten Son into the world to crush that roaring lion; hasten to our call for help, and snatch from ruination, and from the clutches of the noonday devil, this human being made in your image and likeness. Strike terror, Lord, into the beast now laying waste your vineyard. Fill your servants with courage to fight manfully against that reprobate dragon, lest he despise those who put their trust in you, and say with Pharaoh of old: "I know not God, nor will I set Israel free." Let your mighty hand cast him out of your servant, (**_NAME_**), so he may no longer hold captive this person whom it pleased you to make in your image, and to redeem through your Son; who lives and reigns with you, in the unity of the Holy Spirit, God, forever and ever.

All: Amen.

Then he commands the demon as follows: I command you, unclean spirit, whoever you are, along with all your minions now attacking this servant of God, by the mysteries of the incarnation, passion, resurrection, and ascension of our Lord Jesus Christ, by the descent of the Holy Spirit, by the coming of our Lord for judgment, that you tell me by some sign your name, and the day and hour of your departure. I command you, moreover, to obey me to the letter, I who am a minister of God despite my unworthiness; nor shall you be emboldened to harm in any way this creature of God, or the bystanders, or any of their possessions.

Next, he reads over the possessed person these selections from the Gospel, or at least one of them. A reading from the Gospel of John (1:1-14). As he says these opening words he signs himself and the possessed on the brow, lips, and breast. A reading from the Gospel of Mark (16:15-18): At that time Jesus said to His disciples: "Go into all the world and preach the Gospel to every creature. He who believes and is baptized will be saved; but he who does not believe will be condemned. And these signs will follow those who believe: In My name, they will cast out demons; they will speak with new tongues; they will take up serpents; and if they drink anything deadly, it will by no means hurt them; they will lay hands on the sick, and they will recover." A reading from the Gospel of Luke (10:17-20): "Then the seventy returned with joy, saying, "Lord, even the demons are subject to us in Your name." And He said to them, "I saw Satan fall like lightning from Heaven. Behold, I give you the authority to trample on serpents and scorpions, and over all the power of the enemy, and nothing shall by any means hurt you. Nevertheless, do not rejoice in this, that the spirits are subject to you, but rather rejoice because your names are written in Heaven." A reading from the Gospel of Luke (11:14-22): "And He was casting out a demon, and it was mute. So it was, when the demon had gone out, that the mute spoke; and the multitudes marveled. But some of them said, "He casts out demons by Beelzebub, the ruler of the demons." Others, testing Him, sought from Him a sign from heaven. But He, knowing their thoughts, said to them: "Every kingdom divided against itself is brought to desolation, and a house divided against a house falls. If Satan also is divided against himself, how will his kingdom stand? Because you say I cast out demons by Beelzebub. And if I cast out demons by Beelzebub, by whom do your sons cast them out? Therefore, they will be your judges. But if I cast out demons with the finger of God, surely the kingdom of God has come upon you. When a strong man, fully armed, guards his own palace, his goods are in peace. But when a stronger than he comes upon him and overcomes him, he takes from him all his armor in which he trusted, and divides his spoils."

P: Lord, hear my prayer.

All: And let my cry be heard by you.

P: The Lord be with you.

All: May He also be with you.

P: Let us pray. Almighty Lord, Word of God the Father, Jesus Christ, God and Lord of all creation; who gave to your holy apostles the power to trample underfoot serpents and scorpions; who along with the other mandates to work miracles was pleased to grant them the authority to say: "Depart, you devils!" and by whose might Satan was made to fall from heaven like lightning; I humbly call on your holy name in fear and trembling, asking that you grant me, your unworthy servant, pardon for all my sins, steadfast faith, and the power–supported by your mighty arm–to confront with confidence and resolution this cruel demon. I ask this through you, Jesus Christ, our Lord and God, who are coming to judge both the living and the dead and the world by fire.

All: Amen.

Next, he makes the sign of the cross over himself and the one possessed, holds a crucifix in front of the latter's eyes, and, putting his right hand on the latter's head, he says the following in tones filled with confidence and faith:

P: See the cross of the Lord; begone, your hostile powers!

All: The stem of David, the lion of Judah's tribe has conquered.

P: Lord, hear my prayer.

All: And let my cry be heard by you.

P: The Lord be with you.

All: May He also be with you. Let us pray. God and Father of our Lord

Jesus Christ, I appeal to your holy name, humbly begging your kindness, that you graciously grant me help against this and every unclean spirit now tormenting this creature of yours; through Christ our Lord.

All: Amen.

P: I cast you out, unclean spirit, along with every satanic power of the enemy, every specter from Hell, and all your fallen companions; in the name of our Lord Jesus Christ... Begone and stay far from this creature of God! For it is He who commands you, He who flung you headlong from the heights of Heaven into the depths of Hell. It is He who commands you, He who once stilled the sea and the wind and the storm. Hearken, therefore, and tremble in fear, you demon, you enemy of the faith, your foe of the human race, you begetter of death, you robber of life, you corrupter of justice, you root of all evil and vice, seducer of men, betrayer of the nations, instigator of jealousy, fountain of greed, inciter of discord, author of pain and sorrow. Why, then, do you stand and resist, knowing as you must that Christ the Lord brings your plans to nothing? Fear Him, who in Isaac was offered in sacrifice, in Joseph sold into bondage, slain as the paschal lamb, crucified as man, yet triumphed over the powers of Hell. (The three signs of the cross which follow are traced on the brow of the possessed person) ...Begone, then, in the name of the Father, and of the Son, and of the Holy Spirit. Give place to the Holy Spirit by this sign of the holy cross of our Lord Jesus Christ, who lives and reigns with the Father and the Holy Spirit, God, forever and ever.

All: Amen.

P: Lord, hear my prayer.

All: And let my cry be heard by you.

P: The Lord be with you.

All: May He also be with you.

P: Let us pray. God, creator and defender of humans, who made man in your own image, look down in pity on this your servant, (Name), now in the toils of the unclean spirit, now caught up in the fearsome threats of man's ancient enemy, sworn foe of our race, who befuddles and stupefies the human mind, throws it into terror, overwhelms it with fear and panic. Repel, O Lord, the devil's power, break asunder his snares and traps, put the unholy tempter to flight. By the sign (on the brow) of your name, let your servant be protected in mind and body. (The three crosses which follow are traced on the breast of the possessed person). Keep watch over the inmost recesses of his (her) heart; rule over his (her) emotions; strengthen his (her) will. Let the temptations of this mighty enemy vanish from his (her) soul. Graciously grant, O Lord, as we call on your holy name, that the evil spirit, who hitherto terrorized over us, may himself retreat in terror and defeat, so that this servant of yours may sincerely and steadfastly render you the service which is your due; through Christ our Lord.

All: Amen.

P: I command you, ancient serpent, by the judge of the living and the dead, by your Creator, by the Creator of the whole universe, by Him who has the power to consign you to Hell, to leave immediately in fear, along with your

savage subordinate demons, from this servant of
God, <u>Name</u>, who seeks refuge in Jesus and the true church.
I command you again, (on the brow) not by my weakness
but by the might of the Holy Spirit, to depart from this
servant of God, <u>Name</u>, whom almighty God has made in
His image. Yield, therefore, yield not to my own person but
to the minister of Christ. For it is the power of Christ that
forces you, who brought you low by His cross. Tremble
before that mighty arm that broke asunder the dark prison
walls and led forth souls to light. May the trembling that
afflicts this human frame, (on the breast) the fear that
afflicts this image (on the brow) of God, descend on you.
Make no resistance nor delay in leaving this man (woman),
for it has pleased Christ to dwell in man. Do not think of
despising my command because you know me to be a great
sinner. It is God Himself who commands you; the majestic
Christ who commands you. God the Father commands you;
God the Son commands you; God the Holy Spirit
commands you. The mystery of the cross commands you.
The faith of the holy apostles Peter and Paul and of all the
saints commands you. The blood of the martyrs commands
you. The devout prayers of all holy men and women
command you. The saving mysteries of our Christian faith
command you. DEPART, then, transgressor! COME OUT,
you seducer, full of lies and cunning, foe of virtue,
persecutor of the innocent! Give place, abominable
creature, give way, you monster, give way to Christ! For
He has already stripped you of your powers and laid waste
your kingdom, bound you prisoner and plundered your
weapons. He has cast you forth into the outer darkness,
where everlasting ruin awaits you and your allies. To what
purpose do you insolently resist? To what purpose do you
brazenly refuse? We are submitting to God, and resisting
you, so that you will flee from this man (woman). You are
guilty before almighty God, whose laws you have
transgressed. You are guilty before His Son, our Lord Jesus

Christ, whom you presumed to tempt, whom you dared to nail to the cross. You are guilty before the whole human race, whom you enticed to drink from the poisoned cup of death. Therefore, I command you, wasteful dragon, in the name of the spotless Lamb, who has trodden down the viper and the basilisk, and overcome the lion and the dragon, to depart from this man (woman) (on the brow), to depart from the Church of God (signing the bystanders). Tremble and flee, as we call on the name of the Lord, before whom the inhabitants of Hell cower, to whom the heavenly Virtues and Powers and Dominions are subject, whom the Cherubim and Seraphim praise with unending cries as they sing: *Holy, holy, holy, Lord God of Hosts.* The Word made flesh commands you; the Son of God commands you; Jesus of Nazareth commands you, who once, when you despised His disciples, forced you to flee in shameful defeat from a man; and when He had cast you out you did not even dare, except by His leave, to enter a herd of swine. And now as I adjure you in His name, GET OUT of this man (woman) who is His creature. It is useless to resist His will. It is hard for you to kick against the pricks. The longer you delay, the heavier your punishment will be; for it is not men you are despising, but rather Him who rules the living and the dead, who is coming to judge both the living and the dead and the world by fire.

All: Amen.

P: Lord, hear my prayer.

All: And let my cry be heard by you.

P: The Lord be with you.

All: May He also be with you. Let us pray. God of Heaven and earth, God of the angels and archangels, God of the prophets and apostles, God of the martyrs and virgins, God who has power to bestow life after death and rest after toil; for there is no other God than you, nor can there be another true God beside you, the Creator of Heaven and earth, who are truly a King, whose kingdom is without end; we humbly entreat your glorious majesty to *deliver this servant of yours from the unclean spirits; through Christ our Lord.* Amen.

P: Therefore, I command you and every unclean spirit, every spirit from Hell, every satanic power, in the name of Jesus Christ of Nazareth, who was led into the desert after His baptism by John to vanquish you in your fortress, to cease your assaults against the creature whom He has formed from the dust of the earth for His own honor and glory; to shrink with fear at the sight of this man (woman), seeing in him (her) the image of almighty God, rather than his (her) state of human frailty. Yield then to God, who by His servant, Moses, cast you and your malice, in the person of Pharaoh and his army, into the depths of the sea. Yield to God, who, by the singing of psalms on the part of David, His faithful servant, banished you from the heart of King Saul. Yield to God, who condemned you in the person of Judas Iscariot, the traitor. For He now flails you with His divine scourges, He in whose sight you and your legions once cried out: "What have we to do with you, Jesus, Son of the Most High God? Have you come to torture us before the time?" Now He *is* driving you back into the everlasting fire, He who at the end of time will say to the wicked: "Depart from me, you accursed, into the everlasting fire which has been prepared for the devil and his angels." For you, O evil one, and for your followers there will be worms that never die. An unquenchable fire stands ready for you and for your minions, you prince of accursed murderers, father of lust, instigator of blasphemies, model of obscenity, promoter of heresies, inventor of every

profanity. DEPART, then, impious one, DEPART, accursed one, DEPART with all your deceits, for God has willed that man should be His temple. Why do you still linger here? Give honor to God the Father almighty, before whom every knee must bow. Give place to the Lord Jesus Christ, who shed His most precious blood for man. Give place to the Holy Spirit, who by His blessed apostle Peter openly struck you down in the person of Simon Magus; who cursed your lies in Annas and Saphira; who smote you in King Herod because he had not given honor to God; who by His apostle Paul afflicted you with the night of blindness in the magician Elymas, and by the mouth of the same apostle bade you to go out of Pythonissa, the soothsayer. BEGONE, now! BEGONE, seducer! Your place is in solitude; your abode is in the nest of serpents; get down and crawl with them. This matter takes no delay; for see, the Lord, the ruler comes quickly, kindling fire before Him, and it will run on ahead of Him and encompass His enemies in flames. You might delude man, but God you cannot mock. It is He who CASTS YOU OUT, from whose sight nothing is hidden. It is He who repels you, to whose might all things are subject. It is He who EXPELS YOU, He who has prepared everlasting Hell-fire for you and your demons, from whose mouth shall come a sharp sword, who is coming to judge both the living and the dead and the world by fire.
All: Amen.

All the above may be repeated if necessary, until the one possessed has been fully freed.

It will also help to say devoutly and often over the afflicted person the Lord's Prayer, the Apostle's Creed, and the Athanasian Creed.

P: Whoever wills to be saved must before all else hold fast to repentance and faith in the cross.

All: Unless one keeps this faith whole and untarnished, without doubt he will perish forever.

P: Now this is the summary of our faith: that we worship one God in Trinity, and Trinity in unity

All: Neither confusing the Persons one with the other, nor making a distinction in their nature.

P: For the Father is a distinct Person; and so is the Son, and so is the Holy Spirit.

All: Yet the Father, Son, and Holy Spirit possess one Godhead, co-equal glory, coeternal majesty.

P: As the Father is, so is the Son, so also is the Holy Spirit.

All: The Father is uncreated, the Son is uncreated, the Holy Spirit is uncreated.

P: The Father is infinite, the Son is infinite, the Holy Spirit is infinite.

All: The Father is eternal, the Son is eternal, the Holy Spirit is eternal.

P: Yet they are not three eternals, but one eternal God.

All: Even as they are not three uncreated, nor three infinites, but one uncreated and one infinite God.

P: So likewise, the Father is almighty, the Son is almighty, the Holy Spirit is almighty.

All: Yet they are not three almighties, but they are the one Almighty.

P: Thus, the Father is God, the Son is God, the Holy Spirit is God.

All: Yet they are not three gods, but one God.

P: Thus, the Father is Lord, the Son is Lord, the Holy Spirit is Lord.

All: Yet there are not three lords, but one Lord.

P: For just as Christian truth compels us to profess that each Person is individually God and Lord, so does the Christian faith forbid us to hold that there are three gods or lords.

All: The Father was not made by any power; He was neither created nor begotten.

P: The Son is from the Father alone, neither created nor made, but begotten.

All: The Holy Spirit is from the Father and the Son, neither made nor created nor begotten, but He proceeds

P: So there is one Father, not three; one Son, not three; one Holy Spirit, not three.

All: And in this Trinity one Person is not earlier or later, nor is one greater or less; but all three Persons are coeternal and coequal.

P: In every way, then, as already affirmed, unity in Trinity and Trinity in unity is to be worshiped.

All: Whoever, then, wills to be saved must agree with this doctrine of the Blessed Trinity.

P: But it is necessary for everlasting salvation that one also firmly believe in the incarnation of our Lord Jesus Christ.

All: True faith, then, requires us to believe and profess that our Lord Jesus Christ, the Son of God, is both God and man.

P: He is God, begotten of the substance of the Father from eternity; He is man, born in time of the substance of His mother.

All: He is perfect God, and perfect man subsisting in a rational soul and a human body.

P: He is equal to the Father in His divine nature, but less than the Father in His human nature.

All: And though He is God and man, yet He is the one Christ, not two.

P: One, however, not by any change of divinity into flesh, but by the act of God assuming a human nature.

All: He is one only, not by a mixture of substance, but by the oneness of His Person.

P: For, somewhat as the rational soul and the body compose one man, so Christ is one Person who is both God and man;

All: Who suffered for our salvation, who descended into Hell, who rose again the third day from the dead

P: Who ascended into Heaven, and sits at the right hand of God the Father almighty, from there He shall come to judge both the living and the dead.

All: At His coming all men shall rise again in their bodies, and shall give an account of their works.

P: And those who have done good shall enter everlasting life, but those who have done evil into everlasting fire.

All: All this is Christian faith, and unless one believes it truly and firmly one cannot be saved.

P: Glory be to the Father.

All: As it was in the beginning.

[Here follow many psalms which may be used at the exorcist's discretion but are not a necessary part of the rite. Some of them occur in other parts of the Rite and are so indicated; the others may be taken from the Psalter. Psalm 90; psalm 67; psalm 69; psalm 53; psalm 117; psalm 34; psalm 30; psalm 21; psalm 3; psalm 10; psalm 12.]

Prayer Following Deliverance

P: Almighty God, we beg you to keep the evil spirit from further bothering this servant of yours, and to keep him far away, never to return. At your command, O Lord, may the goodness and peace of our Lord Jesus Christ, our Redeemer, take possession of this man (woman). May we no longer fear any evil since the Lord is with us; who lives and reigns with you, in the unity of the Holy Spirit, God, forever and ever.

All: Amen.

CHAPTER 8: ANGELOLOGY-GUARDIANS & PROTECTORS

Angels are believed to be from the realm of God and freely travel around to protect. Their name means the winged messenger. There are millions of angels however I have chosen just a few that are crucial to today.

Abaddon
God's destroyer angel, angel of the bottomless pit and is believed to be the one who cast Satan to the bottomless pit.

Aban
Female yazata angel in Zoroastrianism. She is in the starry region of the sky and looks over month of October.

Abariel
One of the regents of the moon. Invoked in rituals involving emotions.

Abathar Muzania
Always depicted with a set of scales. Weighs the souls of the dead.

Abdiel
Servant of God, has fought Satan, called upon for matter concerning faith in yourself and faith in God.

Abdizuel
Governs the mansions of the moon. Helps in Harvest and plantations to prosper.

Abraxas
A go between God and mankind. Rules the 365 Heavens

Abrinae
Governs the mansions of the moon. Helps married couples and supports soldiers; he hinders government.

Abuliel
Carries prayers to the Throne of God.

Abuzohar
Looks after the moon. Invoked in matters concerning the moon.

Achaiah-Achajah
Guardian angel of people born between April 21-25. Helps people become more patient and accepting.

Acrabiel-Ruling
Angel of the zodiac and responsible for the sign of Scorpio.

Adam
First human, called the bright angel or second angel.

Adimus
Demoted by Catholic Church. Is believed to be condemned by God to eternal damnation.

Adnachiel
In charge of the order of angels. Looks after Sagittarians and the month of November.

Adriel
Rules mansions of the moon. Improves bad fortune and makes love long lasting, also strengthens buildings and assists sailors. In Jewish traditions, he is known as the angel of death.

Aeons
Female symbol of wisdom.

Af
Destroying angel is also known as angel of death.

Afriel

Interest in the young, children and animals. Promotes a positive attitude and a vision of a better world.

Agiel
Angel of Saturn. Invoked by magicians making Saturnine talismans.

Ahura Mazda
Looks after heaven and earth, constantly fighting for the forces of good.

Ahurani
Female yazata angel, looks after water.

Airyaman
Yazata angel responsible for healing and friendship.

Akathrielah Yelod Sabaoth
Powerful angel in Jewish legend. Ranks above all angels and stands at the entrance of Heaven.

Akatriel
Angel-prince who proclaims divine mysteries. Consulted when there is a doubt or mystery that surrounds a problem.

Aker
Will govern the world after the day of judgement.

Akhazriel
Delivers God's pronouncements and passes on important messages.

Akhshti
Yazata angel, he personifies peace.

Aladiah
Angel of barrenness, called upon for cases of infertility. He also is called upon to aid people with mental illness, also improves memories and encourages them to mentally challenged tasks.

Aladiah
Guardian for people born May 6-10, heals people emotionally.

Amael
Ruler of the choir of principalities and is angel of hope. Enjoys working with people who are developing their psychic skills.

Amasras
He enjoys helping farmers and gardeners. Is called upon to increase the potency of magic spells.

Ambriel
Prince of the Order of the Thrones and the ruling angel of May. Wards off evil and negative energies.

Ameretat
Angel of immortality and rules over plants.

Amesha Spentas
Holy immortal who protected the world when it was first created.

Amitiel
Angel of truth. Can be called upon for matters requiring honesty and integrity. Wears white robes and has a large pendant of a cross on his chest. His right hand is held at head height with the first two fingers upraised, his thumb holds the other two fingers in his palm.

Amnediel
Is also one who governs the mansions of the moon. Helps create friendship, love, and happy times for travelers. He also repels mice and imprisons captives.

Amnitziel
Looks after astrological sign of Pisces, and the month of February.

Anabiel
Called upon to cure stupidity

Anafiel
Member of the Sarim, head of the eight principal angels of the Merkabah. He looks after the keys to the palaces of heaven.

Anahel
Ruler of the third heaven but serves in the fourth of the seven heavens.

Anahita
Angel of fertility, helps with matters concerning fertility and pregnancy.

Anamchara
Guardian angel of the ancient celts. Has special interest in people who are developing spiritually, but willing to help anyone in need.

Anauel
Angel of prosperity and commerce, looks after people involved in business or financial matters. Also the angel of people born between January 31st and February 4th, has brown hair and wears green robes. Has small leather or cloth bag in one hand.

Aniel
Is one of the seventy-two Schemhamphoras, group of angels who bear the various names of God found in the Jewish scriptures.

Anixiel
Also governs the mansions of the moon, helps alchemists, hunters, and sailors.

Annan
Angel who helps thunder look after the clouds.

Aral
Angel of fire

Ardifiel
Also governs the mansions of the moon, he strengthens buildings, promotes love and good feelings, and helps oppose enemies.

Ardoustus
Helps people who are trying to nurture someone or something.

Arphugitonos
Will be one of the nine angels to rule after the day of judgement.

Arshtat
Female yazata angel, personifies honesty and justice.

Artiyail
Angel who helps people overcome anxiety, stress, and depression.

Asaliah
Angel of justice. Guardian angel for people born between November 13th and 17th.

Asaph
Angel credited with writing part of the bible, he is chief of the heavenly hosts who endlessly sing God's praises.

Asariel
Planetary Angel, ruler of Neptune. Has task of encouraging people to trust their intuition and act upon it. Looks after people who are clairvoyant and mediumship.

Asha Vahishta
One of the seven Amesha Spentas, ensures that everything in the universe occurs in the correct lawful order. Offers justice and spiritual knowledge to anyone who asks for it.

Ashi Vanghuhi
Female yazata angel, bestows blessings on people who deserve them.

Asman
Male yazata angel, rules over the sky.

Asmodel
Governs the month of April and is responsible for people born under the Taurus sign. Invoked on any matters of love and romance.

Atar
Most important Male yazata angel, he is Angel of fire.

Avartiel
Helps protect pregnant women from miscarriages. Both men and women wear amulets with Avartiel's name to ward off evil.

Avatar
Ten magical beings in Hinduism, intermediaries between God and mankind.

Azbuga
Angel prince in the Sarim and is one of the eight throne angels of judgment. His task is to welcome the worthy into heaven and clothe them with the garment of righteousness.

Azrael
Lives in the third heaven and is responsible for recording everybody's names when they are born and erasing them again when they die. Ruler of Pluto.

Azriel
Helps God watch over the earth.

Badpatiel
Angel who protect women from miscarriage.

Baglis
Helps people overcome addictions and other problems that have the potential to destroy people's lives. Must be called upon during the second hour of the day.

Balthial
Angel of forgiveness. Can be invoked to help in situations when you should forgive someone else but find it difficult to do so. Also helps people overcome feelings of rage, bitterness, jealousy and envy.

Barbelo
Female archon and angel of prosperity and good fortune. Can be invoked when you need more of these qualities in your life.

Barchiel
Ruler of the order of Seraphim, angel of February, prince of third heaven, and leading member of Sarim. Looks after Scorpio's and Pisces. He provides a positive outlook on life and good fortune.

Bariel
One of the princes of the Malakhim. He is one of the angel of Wednesday, and looks after the eleventh hour of every day.

Barman
Looks after the animals on earth, and chief of the thirty angels who looked after each day of the month.

Bath Kol
Considered female, helps people engage in prophecy, Diviners can call out to help understand an omen or intuitions.

Beburos
One of the nine angels who will govern the world after the day of judgment.

Bethnael
Also governs the mansions of the moon, aids expansion and increase, and helps travelers. Encourages divorce when relations are failing.

Bethor
Olympian spirit angel, responsible for the well-being of Jupiter.

Bodhisattvas
Angel like beings in Mahayana Buddhism. Helps people reach salvation.

Boel
One of the seven angels attending the Throne of God. Also looks after the keys to the four corners of the earth.

Botuliel
Responsible for the sign of virgo.

Buddhism Angels
Helps people who are currently alive attain enlightment.

Cahatel
Guardian angel for people born April 26th to 30th.

Caliel
Guardian angel for people born June 16th to 21st. Angel of joy and laughter, also helps people think before acting.

Cambiel
Looks after people under sign of Aquarius.

Cassiel
Angel of solitude and tears, lord of Saturn and sign of Capricorn. Associated with karma, helps people understand the law of cause and effect.

Cerviel
One of the leaders of the choir of principalities.

Chadaqiel
Angel of the sign of Libra.

Chalkydri
Have twelve wings, and sing every morning as the sun rises.

Chamuel
Head of the choir of Dominions. Can be called upon for any matters involving tolerance, understanding, forgiveness and love. You can also call upon him for additional strength or are in conflict with someone else. Provides courage, persistence, and determination.

Charmeine
Angel of joy, happiness, friendship, and love.

Chassan
Angel of Air, assists Archangel Raphael.

Chavakiah
Guardian angel of people born from September 13th to the 17th.

Chayyiel
Angel-prince and member of the Sarim. Leader of the Hayyoth who is responsible for carrying the Throne of God.

Cherub
Small, Chubby, Happy, child-like angel.

Cherubim
They are the second-highest rank of angels in Dionysius' hierarchy of angels.

Chieftains
Describes the seventy guardian angels that look after different peoples of the earth.

Childbed Angels
Looks after mothers during childbirth and protects newly born babies from evil spirits.

Chista
Female yazata, teaches religious instruction.

Choirs
Hierarchy of angels.

Chosetiel
Responsible for the sign of Sagittarius.

Cochabiel
Responsible for the planet Mercury.

Colopatiron
Encourages people to act on their intuition. You can call upon him when trying to develop your psychic abilities.

Daena
Female yazata. Looks after people's consciences, encouraging them to act honestly and ethically.

Dagymiel
Responsible for the sign of Pisces.

Damabiah
One of the seventy-two Schemhamphoras. Guardian angel of people born between February 10th and 14th. Offers the benefit of his wisdom to people who sincerely ask for it.

Day Angels
Angels have been assigned to different days of the week such as: Sunday-Raphael and Michael, Monday-Gabriel, Tuesday-Chamuel, Wednesday-Michael and Raphael, Thursday-Tzaphiel and Sachiel, Friday-Haniel and Anael, Saturday-Tzaphiel and Cassiel.

Deliel
Responsible for the sign of Aquarius.

Destroying Angels
Acts on God's behalf to punish people who deserve it.

Dina
Guardian of the Torah, and has special interest in learning and wisdom.

Djibril
Islamic name of Archangel Gabriel. He is sometimes called the bringer of good news and faithful servant.

Dominions
Fourth most important rank of angels in Dionysius.

Donquel
One of the angels of Venus. Angel of love and romance. Usually called upon men to find a good woman.

Dynamis
Both an aeon and one of the rulers of the archons. He is the personification of divine power.

Ecanus
Helps people who are involved in writing. He can be invoked by people intending to make a career in literary pursuits.

Eiael
One of the seventy-two Schemhamphoras. Angel of both happiness and occult knowledge. Also aids in longevity and positive outlook on life. Guardian angel to those born from February 20th to the 24th.

Elders
Known as the twenty-four angels who sit upon thrones that circle the Throne of God.

Elemiah
Guardian Angel of people born from April 5th to the 9th. Looks after travelers, particularly people traveling over sea. Can be invoked by anyone involved in inner growth and spiritual pursuits.

Elim
Superior class of angels.

Elimiel
Looks after the moon.

Elohim
One of the ten choir angels mentioned in the key of soloman.

Elomnia
Can be invoked to help control losses and to gain money.

Enediel
Also governs the mansions of the moon. Helps people find treasure and aids travelers, involved in agriculture. In medicine he impedes purgatives, also ensures that prisoners are held securely.

Eraziel
Angel of the sign Taurus.

Erelim
Looks after plants and vegetation.

Erellim
Valiant ones.

Erethe
Female yazata, personifies honesty and truth.

Ergediel
Also governs the mansions of the moon, cures the sick and strengthens the bonds of love between married couples. Helps people traveling by sea.

Eth
Angel who looks after time and ensures that everything happens when it should.

Ezekiel
Angel of transformation, helps people turn their lives around and create positive outlook on life.

Ezgadi
Angel who can be invoked for protection while traveling.

Forces
Fourth position, looks after earthly concerns.

Fravashis
Guardian angels that accompany people through life. They can guide and advise, but cannot act directly.

Gabriel
One of the four named archangels, angel of annunciation, angel of mercy, and angel of revelation. He is also mentioned in the bible. Provides good health, education for students, and ensures that travelers return home safely from their journey.

Gabriella
Only female Archangel. Looks after the souls of unborn babies, and teaches them in the womb.

Gabuthelon
One of the nine angels that will govern the world after the day of judgment.

Galgalliel
One of the two that rule the sun. Makes sure sun follows its daily path.

Galgallim
Name for the choir of Thrones.

Gatekeeper Angels
Angels that stand at the gates of heaven.

Gavreel
One of the guardians of the second heaven. Helps create harmony in potentially difficult and stressful situations.

Gazardiel
One of the angels who is responsible for sunrise and sunset. Can be invoked for new beginnings.

Gazriel
Called upon to ensure the success of any enterprise.

Gedobonai
Helps people control any potential financial losses or gains.

Geliel
Also governs the mansions of the moon. Helps cure illnesses and assists prisoners escape.

Gethsemane Angel
The angel who comforted Jesus in the hours before his arrest.

Geush Urvan
Yazata Angel looks after wellbeing of animals.

Godiel
Responsible for the sign of Capricorn.

Graphiel
Angel of Mars.

Guardian Angel
Looks after individuals, churches, cities, and even nations.

Haaiah
Member of the Schemhamphoras, belongs to the choir of the Dominions, and he promotes justice, civility, liberty, and morality. He also is the guardian angel for people born between July 28th and August 1st.

Haamiah
Angel of integrity and a member of the order of powers. He also is one of the members of the Schemhamphoras. He is the guardian angel to people born between September 29th and October 3rd.

Habbiel
Looks after Mondays, has a strong interest in love, loyalty, and commitment. Angel to call upon if you or your partner experience problems in committing. Helps people find trust and openness to commit to each other.

Habujah
Member of the Schemhamphoras, also looks after fertility and agriculture. He is the guardian angel to people born between February 25th and 29th.

Hadraniel
Helps people increase the love they feel to their partners. Call upon him to help express yourself.

Hael
Call upon to send blessings to someone or thank them for their help or kindness.

Hafaza
Islamic equivalent of guardian angels. Instead of having one Muslims have four.

Hagiel
Angel of planet Venus, frequently invoked by magicians when making talismans or performing spells relating to love and romance.

Hagith
Olympian spirit looks after planet Venus.

Hahahel
Member of the Schemhamphoras, guardian angel of people born October 14th to the 18th. Helps sick people regain their health and vitality.

Hahajah
Member of the Schemhamphoras. Guardian angel to people born between May 16th and the 20th, and also July 17th to the 22nd. Angel of health and well-being, and also peace of mind for people who need it.

Hahasiah
Member of the Schemhamphoras, guardian angel to those people born between December 3rd to the 7th. Helps people retain what they have studied.

Hajael
Member of the Schemhamphoras, guardian angel to those people born between March 11th and 15th. Helps people understand complicated ideas and concepts.

Hakamiah
Member of the Cherubim, and is the guardian angel of France. Guardian angel of people born between June 6th and 10th. Provides motivation and help for people who want to progress.

Hamael
Invoked whenever you need to appear calm and dignified. Provides persistence, determination, and practicality.

Hamalatal-'Arsh
In Islam, these are the ones who carry the chair of God. Appear as a man, bull, eagle, and a lion.

Hamaliel
Chief of the choir of virtues and the ruler of August. Archangel for the zodiac sign of Virgo. Invoked for matters of logic and attention to detail.

Hamied
Creates miracles, call on him when need a miracle.

Haniel
One of the rulers of the order of Principalities and is considered one of the ten archangels. Ruler of planet Venus.

Harahel
Member of the Schemhamphoras, responsible for schools, universities, libraries, archives, and other repositories of knowledge. Guardian angel for people born between January 11th and 15th.

Harahil
In Islamic is the angel that looks after dawn every day. Hangs a large white diamond over the eastern horizon. The diamonds work to ensure the proper rotation of the earth.

Hariel
Member of the Chrubim and Schemhamphoras, guardian angel to those people born between June 1st and June 5th.

Haurvatat
Archangel in Zoroastrianism, angel of wholeness and perfection, and rules over water.

Havani
Yazata angel in Zoroastrianism, looks after the period between sunrise and noon every day.

Hayyoth
In Jewish tradition, these group of angels live in the seventh heaven closest to God. Angels of fire.

Haziel
Member of the Cherubim and Schemhamphoras, guardian angel to people born between May 1st and 5th. Invoked when you are seeking God's mercy and compassion, or seeking harmony between groups of people.

Heman
One of the choir directors of the angels that continually praise God. Directs in the morning.

Hizkiel
Archangel Gabriel's assistant in times of wars.

Hodniel
Can be called upon to help cure human stupidity.

Hru
Angel in charge of all secret wisdom.

Huris
In Islamic these are beautiful female angels who provide pleasure to people who have earned eternal happiness by their good deeds on earth.

Hvare
Khshaeta-Yazata angel in Zoroastrianism who rules over the sun.

I AM
One of the most important of the Enochian Angels, possible that she is the supreme being in this system.

Iachadiel
One of the angels of the moon and is sometimes invoked by magicians when performing rituals involving the moon.

Iahhel
Looks after the needs of hermits, philosophers, teachers, and anyone who is studying, invoked to help with meditation and for self-imposed retirement from the world.

Ielahiah
Member of the Schemhamphoras, assists people with matters of justice. Guardian angel to people born October 29th to November 2nd.

Ieliel
Member of the Schemhamphoras, guardian angel to people born between January 6th and 10th.

Iezalel
Guardian to people born between May 21st and 25th. Helps people communicate better.

Isda
Angel of physical, emotional, and spiritual nourishment, also angel of food.

Israfil
Angel who will blow the trumpet on the day of judgement.

Itqal
Works with Archangel Haniel and specializes in resolving disagreements especially with family members. Restores love, affection and consideration of others.

Jabamiah
Assists Archangel Uriel in his work. Member of the Schemhamphoras, guardian angel to those people born between March 6th and 10th. Helps pursue goals.

Jael or Jaoel
Belongs to the choir of Cherubim.

Jajajel
Member of the Schemhamphoras.

Jarahel
Angel responsible for the moon.

Jazeriel
Governs the mansions of the moon. Beneficial angel helps with harvest, journeys, and profit.

Jeduthun
One of the directors of the choirs of angels that continually to praise God.

Jegudiel
Helps anyone who is wanting to form a closer relationship with God.

Jehoel
Angel of the presence, member of the Sarim, and ruler of the order of Seraphim. Happy to help musicians especially singers.

Jehudiel
Responsible for the movements of the planets.

Jehuvajah
Member of the Schemhamphoras.

Jejalel
Member of the Schemhamphoras, guardian angel to those born between July 7th and 11th. Helps self employed people make sound business decisions.

Jelial
Belongs to the order of the Seraphim, interest in stimulating love and passion within existing relationships. Guardian angel to Turkey and of people born between March 26th and 30th.

Jerathel
Member of the Schemhamphoras.

Jeremiel
Possible another name for Archangel Uriel.

Jezalel
Member of the Schemhamphoras.

Joel
Archangel that according to the book of Adam and Eve, led the couple through the Gardens of Eden and asked Adam to name everything he saw.

Jophiel
One of the seven main Archangels, member of the Sarim, ruler of the order of the Thrones. Strong interest in beauty, and can be invoked by anyone involved in creating beauty in any form. Patron angel to the artists.

Kalka'il
Islamic tradition is in charge of the houris in Heaven.

Kerubeem
Islamic equivalent to the Cherubim.

Kerubiel
One leader of the Cherubim.

Kether
One of the ten angels who rule over the holy sephiroth.

Khamael
Archangel of Geburah.

Khshathra Vairya
Archangel in Zoroastrianism who looks after soldiers and people who are poor. Brings prosperity and knowledge of God to those who need it.

Kutiel
Angel who offers help to anyone who dowses for water, oil, gold, or anything else.

Kyriel
Governs the mansions of the moon. Helps people tame wild animals, strengthens prisons, and has the ability to summon people to any place he cares to name.

Labbiel
Archangel Raphael's original name.

Lahabiel
One of the Raphael's chief assistants. Can be invoked to ward off evil of any sort. His name is often inscribed on protective amulets.

Lailah
Jewish angel of Night. Responsible for taking sperm to God so he can decide what sort of person the resulting child be.

Lailiel
Ruler of the Earth and night.

Lecabel
Member of the Schemhamphoras, guardian angel to those born between August 23rd and 28th. Helps people develop their skills and talents.

Lehahiah
Member of the Schemhamphoras, guardian angel to those born between September 8th and 12th.

Lelahel
One of the Seraphim, member of the Schemhamphoras, guardian angel to those born between April 15th and 20th. Called upon for good health and success in worthwhile activities.

Leviah
Member of the Schemhamphoras, guardian angel to those born between June 22nd and 26th. Helps people set goals and work hard to achieve them.

Liwel
Angel of creativity who can be called upon when you have doubts about creative abilities. Also helps lovers develop their relationship.

Machidiel
One of the angels of the tree of life, frequently invoked by people performing love magic. Angel of March, looks after those born under the sign of Aries. Helps people express their love to others.

Madimiel
Angel responsible for the planet Mars.

Mahasiah
Member of the Schemhamphoras, guardian angel to those born between April 10th and 14th.

Maion
Ruler of the planet Saturn, helps people who work hard achieve their goals. Invoke whenever you need self-control or self-discipline.

Malahidael
Invoked whenever you need necessary courage to stand up for what you believe is right.

Malashiel
Friday Angel who lives in the Third Heaven.

Malkhidael
Archangel for the sign of Aries and rules the month of March.

Malkiel
One of the three angelic princes in the Kabbalah. Promises success to people who are persistent and work hard.

Manadel
Member of the Schemhamphoras, guardian angel to those born between February 15th and 19th.

Maonghah
Yazata angel in Zoroastrianism who rules over the moon.

Masleh
Angel in charge of the zodiac.

Masniel
One of the ruling angels of the zodiac and is responsible for the sign of libra.

Matariel
One of the rulers of the Earth and is responsible for rain.

Mebahel
Member of the Schemhamphoras, guardian angel of those born between May 26th and 31st. Encourages friendship and conversations.

Mebahiah
Member of the Schemhamphoras, guardian angel of those born between December 22nd and 26th. Strong interest in philosophy and ethics.

Mediator Angels
Listens to people's prayers and delivers them to God.

Meher
Yazata Angel of light, mercy, and justice.

Mehiel
Guardian angel to those born between February 5th and 9th.

Mehikiel
Member of the Schemhamphoras.

Melahel
Member of the Schemhamphoras, nurturing and protective angel, guardian angel to those born between July 12th and 16th.

Melchizedek
Belongs to the order of Virtues. Angel of presence, and one of the most powerful angels in Heaven.

Melek Ta'us
Known as the Peacock angel and is main Archangel in the belief system of the Yazidis.

Menadel
Member of the Schemhamphoras, guardian angel to those born between September 18th and 23rd.

Meniel
Member of the Schemhamporas.

Metatron
Chancellor of Heaven, member of Sarim, and one leader of the Seraphim. Call upon when you are engaged in deep thought.

Micah
Dedicated to the spiritual growth of mankind. Invoke if you are pursuing spiritual growth.

Michael
God's most important warrior angel. Fights for everything good, honorable and righteous.

Mihael
Angel of fertility and fidelity. Guardian angel to those born between November 18th and 22nd. Invoked for happiness and ensure loyalty and faithfulness.

Mihr
Angel of business relationships.

Mikael
Guardian angel to those born between October 19th and 23rd. Angel of prosperity and well-being.

Mikhail
One of the four Archangels in Islam.

Miniel
Can be invoked to induce passion in even the most reluctant woman.

Mithra
Angel of light in Zoroastrianism. Mediates between mankind and God and helps judge the souls of people when they die.

Mizrael
In Kabbalah, considered an Archangel. Member of the Schemhamphoras, guardian angel to those born between January 16th and 20th.

Mumijah
Member of the Schemhamphoras, guardian angel of those born between March 16th and 20th. Provides motivation for those who ask.

Munkar
Islamic angels of mercy.

Muriel
Archangel responsible for the sign of Cancer, and looks after the month of July. Can be invoked whenever emotions need to be kept under control.

Nabo
Records the good and bad deeds of humankind.

Nairyosangha
Yazata angel in Zoroastrianism who serves as messenger for Ahura Mazda.

Nakhiel
Angel of the sun, helps Michael look after the sun.

Nakir
Islamic angel of mercy. Task is to ask people in their graves about their faith.

Nanael
Belongs to the choir of Principalities and a member of the Schemhamporas. Guardian angel to those born between December 13th and 16th. Helps people involved in law and order.

Nathanael
Prince of the Seraphim.

Nathanel
Jewish legend is one of the angels of fire.

Neciel
Governs the mansions of the moon, responsible for Azobra, helps travelers and people engaged in business.

Nemamiah
Has strong interest in just causes, member of the Schemhamphoras. Guardian angel to those born between January 1st and 5th. Invoke when seeking justice.

Nilaihah
Belonging to the choir of Dominions, angel of harmony and beauty, can help people find love and happiness, especially after setback or disappointment.

Nithhaja
Member of the choir of Dominions, member of the Schemhamphoras, and guardian angel to those born between July 23rd and 27th. Encourages love, happiness and friendship.

Nogahel
Responsible for the planet Venus.

Nuriel
Angel of fire and hail. Strong force against evil.

Och
One of the seven Olympian spirits who rule over the 196 divisions of Heaven. Responsible for the sun, and is willing to help anyone who desires knowledge.

Omophorus
In Manichaean belief, carried the entire world on his shoulders.

Ongkanon
Willing to help people express their inner most feelings, especially concerning love.

Ooniemme
Called upon whenever you feel grateful and whenever you wish to bless someone.

Ophaniel
One of the leaders of the Cherubim. Ruler of the Earth, and is in charge of the phases of the moon.

Ophiel
One of the seven Olympian spirits who rule over the 196 divisions of the Heaven. Responsible for the planet Mercury.

Orifiel
Member of the choir of the Thrones. Angel of Saturn.

Pahaliah
Member of the Schemhamphoras, and guardian angel to those born between June 27th and July 1st. Encourages people to be honest, upright and fair.

Pakhiel
Angel of the sign Cancer, and helps Archangel Muriel look for people under this sign.

Parendi
Female Yazata angel in Zoroastrianism for abundance.

Penuel
Archangel and angel of the presence. Angel of Repentance.

Perpetiel
Invoked if you are working on a worthwhile project and finding it hard to accomplish. Helps achieve success.

Phaleg
Rules the order of the Angels. Responsible for the planet Mars.

Phorlach
Angel of the element earth.

Phul
One of the seven Olympian Spirits who rule over the 196 sections of Heaven. Responsible for the moon.

Polial
Member of the choir of Principalities and Schemhamphoras. Guardian angel to those born between December 27th and 31st.

Pravuil
Archangel who keeps the celestial records.

Puriel
Angel of Punishment. He examines all the souls that enters Heaven to ensure they meet his high standards, ruthless in dealing with the wicked.

Qaddism
Holy Ones who stand with the watchers on either side of the Throne of God.

Quelamia
One of the seven who surround the Throne of God.

Ra'amiel
Belongs to the rulers of the earth.

Ra'ashiel
Belongs to the rulers of the earth, and is responsible for earthquakes.

Racheil
Belongs to the choir of Ophanim and is the ruler of Venus. Invoked for help in love and sexuality.

Rachmiel
Angel of mercy, invoked for help during childbirth.

Radueriel
Celestial archivist, believed to be the wisest angel in Heaven. Invoked to those who seek wisdom and insight.

Rahab
Angel of the sea.

Rahatiel
In Jewish tradition is one of the rulers of the earth and is responsible for looking after the constellations and stars.

Rahmiel
Angel of mercy, compassion and love. Called upon for people who lack love and compassion.

Raman
Yazata angel in Zoroastrianism who is responsible for joy and happiness.

Rapithwin
Yazata angel in Zoroastrianism looks after the hours from noon to 3 pm.

Rasanstat
Female Yazata angel in Zoroastrianism who encourages truth and honesty in all undertakings.

Rata
Female Yazata angel in Zoroastrianism who encourages charity and helpfulness.

Raziel
Member of the Cherubim, and strong interest in magic and knowledge.

Rahael
Belongs to the choir of Powers and is the angel of longevity. Member of the Schemhamphoras, and is the angel of self-respect. Can be invoked for matters of health, self-respect and respect for others. Guardian angel to those born between October 4th and 8th.

Rajajel
Belongs to the choir of Dominions, member of the Schemhamphoras, and guardian angel for those born between August 13th and 17th.

Remiel
Angel of divine vision. One of the seven Archangels who attend the Throne of God. Happy to help anyone who needs to see into the future.

Requiel
Governs the mansions of the moon. Helps sick people regain their health.

Ridwan
Islamic tradition is the angel who stands at the entrance to Heaven.

Rikbiel
Member of the choir of Cherubim, Prince of the Merkabah, and a member of the Sarim.

Rochel
Angel of lost property and can be invoked when anything is misplaced or lost. Guardian angel to those born between March 1st and 5th.

Rubiel
Invoked by people participating in games of chance.

Ruchiel
One of the rulers of the earth and responsible for the wind.

Sabath
One of the two angels who rule the sixth heaven. Rules daytime hours.

Sabathiel
In Jewish Kabbalah, angel responsible for the planet Saturn.

Sachiel
Archangel of Jupiter and member of the Cherubim.

Sagnessagiel
Prince of wisdom. Provides wisdom, knowledge, and understanding and also patience and forgiveness.

Sahaqiel
One of the seven great Archangels.

Samandiriel
Angel of fertility.

Samaqiel
Angel of the sign Capricorn and helps look for people born under this sign.

Sandalphon
Archangel who is head of the guardian angels.

Santriel
Angel who collects the bodies of men and women who failed to honor the Sabbath while they were alive.

Saraqael
Angel of presence.

Sariel
One of the seven Archangels, angel of presence and member of the Sarim. Looks after people born under the sign of Aries.

Saritaiel
Angel of Sagittarius and helps look for people born under this sign.

Sataniel
Ruling angel of zodiac and is responsible for sign of Cancer.

Sayitziel
Angel of Scorpio and helps look for people born under this sign.

Scheliel
Governs the mansions of the moon. Helps friends and lovers and people engaged in making a profit.

Sealiah
Member of the Schemhamphoras, and guardian angel to people born between November 3rd and 7th. Provides happiness and good health to people who ask for it.

Sealtiel
Special interest in meditation, contemplation, spirituality, and worship.

Sedekiah
Invoked by prospectors and people searching for hidden treasure.

Seheliel
Angel who helps people gain their desires, also provides unlimited energy when necessary.

Sehijah
Member of the Schemhamphoras, and guardian angel to those born between August 7th and 12th. Looks after people far from home.

Semeliel
In Jewish Kabbalah, angel responsible for the sun.

Seraph
Member of the choir of Seraphim.

Seraphiel
One of the leaders of the Seraphim, who teaches those to sing the praises of God.

Serayel
Angel of Gemini and helps look for those born under this sign.

Shalgiel
One of the rulers of the earth, responsible for snow and blizzards.

Shamshiel
In Jewish tradition, one of the rulers of the earth and is responsible for daylight.

Sharhiel
Angel of the sign of Aries, looks after the month of March.

Sharahil
Islamic tradition, angel who looks after the nighttime hours.

Shelachel
Angel of the moon.

Shelathiel
Angel of virgo and looks for people who are born under this sign.

Shemuil
Member of the Sarim

Shen
Chinese angels

Shepherd
One of the six angels of repentance.

Sheratiel
Angel of Leo, also looks for people born under this sign.

Sidriel
Archangel in charge of the First Heaven.

Sirael
Member of the choir of Seraphim, also a member of Schemhamphoras. Guardian angel for those born between April 1st and 4th. Helps people combine idealism, thought and practicality to start new adventures.

Sizouse
In Persia, was angel who presided over prayers and delivered them to God.

Sopheriel Mehayye
In Jewish lore, member of Sarim. Looks after the books of the dead and records everyone's date of death.

Sopheriel Memeth
In Jewish lore, member of Sarim. Looks after the books of the living and records who is alive.

Soqed Hozi
In Jewish lore, member of the choir of Thrones, and a Sarim angel prince. Looks after the scales that weighs the human souls.

Spenta Armaiti
In Zoroastrianism, angel of devotion. In charge of the earth and looks after people who care for the earth. Invoked when it is important to determine the truth of the matter.

Splenditenes
Supported the Heavens on his back.

Sstiel YHWH
One of the most important Merkabah angels.

Suriel
Archangel who taught Moses and is responsible for the sign of Taurus.

Tagas
In charge of the angelic choirs that constantly sing God's praise.

Tagriel
One of the chief guards in the Second or Seventh Heaven. Governs the mansions of the moon and is responsible for the health of prisoners.

Tahariel
Angel of Chastity and purification. Encourages cleanliness of mind and body.

Taliahad
Angel who helps Archangel Gabriel look after the element water.

Tarshish
Prince of the choir of Virtues and one of the rulers of Malakhim.

Teiazel
Angel who looks after writers, artists, sculptors and musicians.

Teletiel
Responsible for the sign of Aries.

Teoael
Member of the choir of the Thrones. Invoked to help new business ventures.

Terathel
Guardian angel of those who are born between April 2nd and 6th. Member of the Dominions, and is angel of joy, laughter and optimism.

Tezalel
Angel responsible for trust and fidelity in all loving relationships. Keeps couples together as long as there is a good chance of saving the relationship.

Theliel
Angelic prince of love. Invoked to help men bring love to their lives.

Thunder
Islamic tradition, Angel who looks after the clouds.

Tir
Yazata angel in charge of Mercury and the month of June.

Tiriel
Helps Raphael look after the planet Mercury. Invoked when making talismans relating to Mercury.

Tomimiel
Responsible for the sign of Gemini.

Tsaphiel
One of the angels of the moon, invoked by magicians when performing rituals involving the moon.

Tzakmaqiel
Angel of Aquarius, and helps look for people born under this sign.

Tzaphiel
Looks after Thursdays and Saturdays.

Umbael
Member of the Schemhamphoras, and guardian angel to those born between January 21st and 25th.

Uriel
Archangel of the prophecy. Overseer of Hell who will destroy the gates of hell on judgment day.

Urpaniel
Angel in Judaism who is occasionally used on protective amulets.

Ushahi
Yazata angel in Zoroastrianism who looks after the hours from midnight to dawn every day.

Uzerin
Yazata angel in Zorastrianism who looks after the hours of 3pm till sunset every day.

Uzziel
Angel of mercy, stands at the Throne of God.

Vakhabiel
Angel of Pisces, and looks for people born under this sign.

Valoel
Provides peace, contentment, and understanding.

Vasiariah
Belongs to the Dominions, looks after justice, lawyers, judges, and courts of law. Invoked for matters of justice, honesty, and fairness.

Vayu
Yazata angel in Zoroastrianism, responsible for wind and air.

Vehael
Member of the Principalities, and member of the Schemhamphoras. Guardian angel to those born between November 23rd and 27th.

Vehujah
In the Kabbalah, member of the Seraphim, and guardian angel for those born between March 21st and 25th.

Verchiel
Regents of the choir of powers. Responsible for the sign of Leo and the month of July. Prince of the choir of Virtues. Call upon for difficulties with family or good friends.

Verethraghna
Yazata angel of success and victory. Is the strongest and fastest, works for honesty and kindness punishes evil-doers.

Vevaliah
Member of the choir of Virtues, and member of the Schemhamphoras. Guardian angel of those born between October 24th and 28th.

Vohu Manah
Leading Amesha Spentas in Zoroastrianism. Angel of self-worth, love, and divine wisdom.

Yahriel
One of the angels of the moon and is sometimes invoked by magicians when performing rituals involving the moon.

Yefifiyyah
Angel of the presence and a member of the Sarim.

Yehudiah
Angel of bereavement and can be called upon for comfort when a loved one dies. Guardian angel to those born between September 3rd and 7th.

Yophiel
Jewish angel of beauty.

Za'amiel
One of the rulers of the earth and responsible for vehemence.

Za'aphiel
One of the rulers of the earth and is responsible for hurricanes and storms. Sometimes deals with evil-doers.

Zachariel
Archangel, Dominions and Powers. Invoked to help people improve their memory.

Zadkiel
Ruler of Jupiter, regent of Sagittarius, ruler of the fifth heaven, member of Sarim, chief of choir of Dominions.

Zamael
Archangel of the planet Mars and looks after Tuesday.

Zamyat
Female Yazata angel in Zoroastrianism who rules over the earth.

Zaphiel
Member of the Cherubim and looks after the planet Saturn.

Zaphkiel
Prince of the choir of Thrones. Looks after the planet Saturn.

Zarall
Member of the Cherubim.

Zebul
One of the rulers of the Sixth Heaven. Rules nighttime hours.

Zebuleon
One of the nine angels that will govern the world after day of judgment.

Zi'iel
One of the rulers of the earth, and responsible for ground tremors and commotion.

Ziqiel
One of the rulers of the earth, and responsible for comets.

Zuriel
Prince regent of the choir of Principalities. Archangel of the sign of Libra and ruler of September.

CHAPTER 9: HOW TO COLLECT PARANORMAL EVIDENCE

Being a paranormal investigator entails a lot more than just traipsing around an allegedly haunted building in the dark hoping to see a ghost. The largest part of your job as an investigator is to document and catalog evidence to substantiate the claims of a haunting, or, in the absence of such evidence, debunk claims of an alleged haunting.

Throughout the investigation process, which we will outline in the next chapter, it will be your responsibility to gather evidence. The process by which we gather evidence is wrought with threats of contamination which can render your evidence obsolete so it is important to go into an investigation armed with the knowledge of how to capture the best evidentiary support.

Collecting Photographic Evidence
1. Take baseline pictures of the entire property (inside and outside) prior to beginning the investigation and going lights-out. Capture as much within the frame of the picture as possible. You will use the baseline pictures to potentially debunk any anomalies within pictures taken during the course of the investigation. What could look like an apparition in a photo taken in a dark room could very well be a wall decoration that is more visible in the baseline photo.
2. Avoid taking pictures in rooms where other investigators are walking about, taking pictures, or have cameras/video equipment setup with infrared external light sources. People walking about can create false positives within photographic evidence whereas IR lamps can create lens flare or other photographic anomalies. If you happen to take

photos under these circumstances, be sure to document the fact that environmental contamination was present.
3. Take more than one picture of each spot. Use a three-picture burst or be fast on the shutter release. If you capture something, you want to try to capture more than one image of it. Using a three-picture burst allows the camera to snap three pictures in rapid-fire succession thereby increasing the possibility that you will have more than one picture with the anomaly present.
4. If you capture an anomaly within a photograph, attempt to recreate it in subsequent photos by any means necessary. Attempt to create motion blur by lowering the camera in mid-capture or ensure that your camera strap is caught within a picture to recreate light strands/rods. If you are able to recreate an image the evidence has to be discounted as of natural occurrence, not supernatural. It should be noted that due to dust and insect presence, orbs are not proof of paranormal activity. It is next to impossible to discern dust particles from "orbs", therefore they must be removed from consideration altogether.
5. Ensure that your camera's lens is free of contaminants such as dust and fingerprints. The presence of contaminants on a camera lens can result in false positives.
6. Ensure if you have long hair that you keep it pulled back and secured to prevent hair entering the photograph and creating an anomaly.
7. Trust your gut. If you get an urge to snap a picture in a certain direction or point of interest, take the picture. Many times, our instincts are alerting us to the presence of something we can't see with the naked eye.

8. Avoid snapping pictures of shiny/reflective surfaces such as windows and mirrors or laminated desktops and furniture. A flash reflection can cause false positives.
9. As you take pictures, be sure to invite any spirits who might be present to come forward. Assure them that you won't harm them and that the camera is safe and not to be feared. Keep in mind, your technology can be intimidating to spirits who may have passed before the advent of cameras, let alone digital ones.
10. Be aware of anyone smoking within the vicinity of your photo session. Also, be aware of visible breath if photographing in the cold. Both cigarette smoke and visible breath can result in false positive evidence.

Collecting Video Evidence

1. Before lights out, baseline videography should be conducted of the property/room where recording will take place. This will help eliminate potential false positives during evidence review sessions.
2. Video evidence may be collected via a mobile or stationary video camera. If stationary ensure that the camera is positioned to capture as much of the room as possible. If mobile, keep the camera as steady as possible to eliminate artifacting.
3. If mobile; pan slowly, refrain from sudden movements, and do not run while holding the camera.
4. If you are using an IR source to capture video in the dark, do not point a flashlight or other IR source at the camera. This can burn out the image and cause false positives.

5. If you are using a stationary camera, you (and teammates) should announce themselves as they enter the room where the camera is placed. They should refrain from whispering while recording is taking place. Speak at regular volume to prevent being confused for paranormal activity/EVP.
6. If you or a teammate cause noise contamination (clears throat, coughs, knocks something over, etc, they should announce it was them and indicate the time at which the occurrence took place. This will prevent false positives in evidence review. Doing this is commonly referred to as "tagging".
7. Announce the time and location of the recording at the beginning of the video session and announce the time at the stop of the video session.
8. Using IR lamps or other external IR/UV/Full Spectrum light sources can cause artifacting in other video cameras/photographic devices. Be aware of the presence of these light sources when conducting photography/videography in the presence of video cameras.

Collecting Environmental Evidence

1. Environmental evidence refers to temperature flux (increase/decrease in basal temperature), increase or decrease in the level of electromagnetic fields (EMF) present in the room, and changes in barometric pressure.
2. Before beginning your investigation, basal readings (often called baselines) should be established and documented. Collect temperature readings, EMF readings, and barometric readings (if your devices can do so) of the outside and inside of the house. Document the readings in a notebook ensuring you are labeling the rooms accordingly.

3. Take note of position of fuse box/circuit breakers, exposed wiring, areas of naturally occurring high EMF, drafts, open windows and doors. Document these in a notebook to have at your disposal during evidence review.
4. During an investigation, should you encounter a cold spot, use a digital ambient thermometer to determine if there is a difference between the cold spot and the surrounding area. Take pictures or video of the display as you move the thermometer from the cold spot to other unaffected areas of the room. Ensure there is no AC vent or other natural source for the cold spot.
5. For changes in EMF, be sure to document the readings with either photographic or video evidence of the detector. Record the changes in a notebook as well. Ensure that the changes are not as result of exposed wiring, external power source, or other natural occurrence.
6. Naturally occurring high levels of EMF (from electronic devices, HVAC, exposed or improperly grounded wiring) should be discussed with the home/business owner as ongoing exposure can result in sensitivity to EMF and manifest feelings of dread, panic, paranoia, nausea, and other feelings that can be confused with the sensation of a paranormal presence.

Collecting Audio Evidence

1. During an investigation, you should attempt to engage spirits and get them to respond to vocal commands and questions. You can capture responses using video and audio equipment. The most popular tool used to collect audio evidence is a digital voice recorder.

2. Audio evidence capture should be conducted in relatively short segments of 15 minutes or less to ensure an easy and non-exhausting review process.
3. At the start of each audio-capture session, you should announce the date, time, and location of the session as well as the names of any team members present. Each team member should speak their name so that their voices are captured on the recording. This will help you identify who is captured on the recording during evidence review.
4. Do not whisper during audio-recording sessions, everyone should speak in normal speaking volumes. Whispering can result in false positives during evidence review.
5. Invite any spirits who might be present to speak into the device, let them know what the voice recorder is and that it is not harmful to them.
6. Be sure to tag any naturally occurring phenomenon such as noise generated by you or teammates, cars passing outside, dogs barking, etc… Tag it with the time of the occurrence as well as the cause of the noise.
7. Conduct EVP sessions separately from other audio evidence collection.

EVP as Audio Evidence

Electronic Voice Phenomenon, or EVP, is an occurrence during a paranormal investigation whereupon a disembodied voice is captured on a voice recorder, either analog (cassette required) or digital (no cassette required).

The voices are not audible during the investigation and are only revealed when the EVP sessions are reviewed.

The phenomenon is greatly debated by the scientific

community and written off as ambient noise captured by the sensitive microphones on the recording devices.

Within the community of paranormal investigators, EVPs are the most abundant of evidence of a haunting. A classification system is widely used to catalog EVP types.

Class A EVP:
A clear and distinct voice or sound that is universally accepted and undisputed, because it must be understood by anyone with normal hearing and without being told or prompted to what is being said or heard. It can be heard without the use of headphones.

Class B EVP:
A voice or sound that is distinct and fairly loud. This class of voice is more common and can be heard by most people after being told what to listen for. It is usually audible to experienced persons who have learned the skill of listening to EVP. It can sometimes be heard without the use of headphones.

Class C EVP:
A faint and whispery voice or sound that can barely be heard and is sometimes indecipherable and unintelligible. It may have paranormal characteristics, such as a mechanical sound. Most investigators would apply objectivity and disregard it, but may save it for reference purposes.

In addition to the classification system currently employed by most groups, many break the EVPs into *events* based on the distinct characteristics of the EVP captured.

These events are:

Morph
The voice and/or words of someone who is speaking is changed into something else in the playback of the recording. Words that are different from the person who spoke, or one voice changing to another, etc...

ERV (event related voices)
Events such as someone talking, coughing, or the sounds of a passing train or car, etc. seems to trigger the EVP.

TR (thread related)
Where an utterance is a comment on, or a response to, an utterance just before. They are related by contextual thread. Examples would be hearing two or more voices talking to each other, as well as a voice responding to something previously said by itself and/or someone or something else.

Capturing EVP Evidence

The process is simple but varies depending on personal preference. One simply has to find a quiet space in an alleged haunted location (or you can see if spirits are willing to communicate with you by performing an EVP session anywhere.)

Once you have found the ideal location, simply turn on your digital voice recorder and start asking questions.

Always announce the date, time and location of your session along with the names of anyone else present.

Have the people present state their names loudly enough to be captured on the recording, that way if you hear the voice later in the recording upon review you know that it is from someone in your group and not from an otherworldly source.

"This is Michael and we are recording EVP session 1 at a private residence in Springfield, Missouri. The date and time is (insert date and time).

With me are (state name of each member of your team and have them say their name out loud)."

During your questioning make sure that you tag any natural sounds so that you do not mistake them for EVPs when you review your session.

Examples of tags would be:

1) A car just passed by
2) Someone in the group coughed
3) My stomach just rumbled, etc…

Any natural environmental noise needs to be tagged.

Do not whisper if you must talk to other group members. Conversation should be at a normal volume so as not to misinterpret the whisper as a voice of a spirit when reviewing your session.

Keep sessions short and do not provoke the spirits. If they want to talk to you they will. Keep in mind, you are trying to contact people who have passed on and choose to stick around for one reason or another. Treat them with respect, be conversational and approachable.

Some common questions to ask are:

1) Is there anyone here who wishes to communicate with us?
2) What is your name?
3) How old are you?
4) Do you know what year it is?
5) Who is the President of the United States?
6) Why do you stay here?
7) Do you know anyone's name in this room?
8) Are you aware that you are dead?
9) What year did you die?
10) How did you die?

You can ask any questions you want as long as you remain personable and respectful. If you think you know the name of the ghost haunting the location you can call them by their name.

When you review your evidence do so in a quiet area free of distractions.

Have a pen and notepad nearby. It is during this crucial review process that you will be glad you kept the sessions short. Listen carefully using headphones/earphones and if you think you found a response to a question or an EVP write down the time within the recording the response happened so that you can go back to it later.

If you are using audio editing software, refrain from excessive filtering and editing as too many modifications can take a natural sound or ambient noise and morph it into a false positive.

When having others listen to your EVPs do not tell them what you think the EVP says, the power of suggestion can lead to a person hearing what you suggested and could result in a false positive. Let others listening know at what point the EVP happens and get their feedback. If they hear what you thought was being said without being prompted then chances are you have a legitimate EVP.

This is a capsule view of the world of EVP. There are many websites out there with great information about Electronic Voice Phenomena. Google the search term "EVP" and read as much as you can about the process, listen to real-life examples, and prepare to be mystified at this amazing glimpse into the afterlife and the spirits that occupy it who are constantly reaching out to us.

White Noise Use

White noise is the random non-descript static sound produced by various electronic devices. The sound covers and combines all wavelengths and frequencies. In this way, it is like the color white which is really a combination of all colors. Hence the name white noise – the combination of all sounds.

Examples of common white noise sources are the radio or television static when set to an empty channel, the hum of an electric fan motor, and the babbling sound of a fast-moving stream or brook.

There are two theories on the use of white noise for EVP ghost investigations:

Theory 1

Using white noise during EVP sessions relies on the random sound reorganization theory of EVP formation.

That theory holds that entities take sounds in the ambient environment and somehow reorganize them into coherent words for us to hear. By providing a white noise source (or at least investigating near a white noise source) you are providing a base of raw sound ("raw material") for the entity to use to form communication.

However, a significant drawback to using this technique is that the white noise can be hard to filter out later when you analyze your recordings and can thus contaminate an otherwise good EVP recording.

White noise can be made from many sources. As previously mentioned, a radio set to an empty channel, an electric fan or similar motor, the babbling of a stream or a running faucet are all good sources of white noise. Additionally, there are white noise generators available (often sold as sleep aids) and software that will generate a white noise signal from a PC.

Theory 2

This theory is that white noise can be used to filter out background noise or enhance EVPs when listening to recordings.

To use white noise in this manner, place the EVP recorder on one side of you and the white noise source on the other side. Stand (or sit) in the middle and turn both on. As you listen to the recording the white noise source will either filter out background noise on the recording and/or enhance any EVPs captured.

There is some evidence this may work. Noise canceling headphones is based on a similar principle. These types of headphones play low levels of white noise through the speakers to filter out surrounding noise and enhance the quality of the audio. Some EVP researchers and paranormal investigators use noise canceling headphones and find them very helpful.

CHAPTER 10: THE INVESTIGATION

Ultimately, how you choose to investigate is up to you. Finding out what works and what doesn't is all part of the process of running your own paranormal investigation organization. With that said though, we can leverage our many years of experience to provide you with a roadmap for success and help you start off on a tried and true formula.

Your Team

A ghost hunting team is made up of key roles which are important for the overall workflow and organization of the team. The following is a high-level breakdown of how you should build your organization.

Director of Investigations
This is typically the founder of the organization or someone the founder entrusts with the day to day operations of the organization. The director is responsible for fielding calls, making inquiries, building the team, conducting training, and being the main point of contact for all activity within the organization.

Team Leader
If the Director is looked at as the CEO of the organization, team leaders are to be looked at as the manager of the individual teams they lead. A team leader is responsible for the protection and leadership of their teams during an investigation and to ensure teams adhere to codes of conduct and organizational by-laws about reporting, evidence review, and client satisfaction. The team lead is the one who team members and clients will turn to with questions and concerns during the investigation.

Second in Command
This role is comparable to a team supervisor within the corporate world. The Second in Command reports directly to the team leader and is responsible for enforcing the directives of upper leadership (Team Leader and Director of Investigations). This role ensures that all guidelines are being met within the course of an investigation and to ensure the investigation stays on course.

Tech Manager
Responsible for the maintenance, care, and appropriate use of team equipment. This individual is responsible for ensuring equipment is functional, set up appropriately, and charged. Upon completion of an investigation, the tech manager is responsible for breaking down the setup, appropriate stowage of equipment, and ensuring that all equipment belonging to the organization is accounted for.

Researcher/Historian
Responsible for research relating to the property and persons connected with the property. Reports to the team leader any data pertinent to the investigation such as known deaths, tragedies, and dates/information of historical significance.

Investigators
These team members are the soldiers, the front line. They are entrusted to carry out investigations of alleged paranormal activity, to gather evidence to support the claims or debunk the claims of paranormal activity, and to conduct themselves in a manner that reflects positively on the organization. They report to the team leader from whom they receive their directives.

Securing an Investigation
For those just starting out in the field of paranormal investigations, you will most likely have to pay your dues by investigating public access areas. These are areas that are open to the public such as parks, historic landmarks, hotels, museums, etc. When first starting out you will most likely have to investigate during regular business hours, or actually be a paying guest at a hotel should you want to investigate claims of a haunting during the late-night hours.

As your team matures you will gain public recognition and ultimately, people will reach out to you to conduct investigations on an invite basis.

When an individual or a company reaches out to your organization with a request to investigate their property, there are some basic courtesies to be extended and a general template to be followed when asking questions of your contact.

1. Remember, that despite the absurdity of a claim, it is real to your contact. They have reached out to you for help because they are scared and don't have any other recourse. Respect each potential client. If you do not earn their trust and take care of them, another group will.

2. Evaluate every caller thoroughly. You are under no obligation to handle every case that comes your way. Over time you will develop an instinct as to whether a claim is legitimate or simply someone seeking attention. Don't be afraid to involve other members of your team in the decision-making process.

3. Take the time to research your clients. Do not walk into a property ill-informed. Research the property

thoroughly including historical records (was there a event of historical significance that could lend credence to a haunting?). See if there has been a reported death on the grounds or in the actual structure by searching the internet, looking over archived newspaper articles, obituaries, or run buy a subscription to an aggregator site such as www.diedinhouse.com which will return any known results of a death in a house.

4. Don't be afraid to ask the client the tough questions. It is okay to ask them if they or anyone in the house has a history of mental illness or chemical dependency. It is your job as an investigator to rule out any natural causes for claims of a haunting before you start looking for supernatural causes.

5. Conduct a thorough interview with the client over the phone. If you want a better feel for the client and the validity of their claims, meet them in a public place to ask further questions Sometimes you can get a better sense of the validity of a claim when you can see the body language of a potential client. Here are some questions you can ask the potential client:

- Do you believe in ghosts?
- Up until this incident, have you previously encountered the paranormal?
- Are you currently on any prescription drugs, OTC drugs, or supplements?
- Are you currently under the care of a psychiatrist or psychologist?
- Do you have a history of alcohol/drug abuse?
- Have you experienced blackouts or missing/unaccounted for time?

- What is your religion if you practice one?
- Have you been hypnotized for any reason in the past?
- Have you used any of the following items: Tarot cards, Ouija boards, talismans, or summoned any spirits?
- Have you brought into your home any earth, rocks, plants, sand, etc... from foreign countries?
- Are any of your friends or acquaintances pagans/Satanists/witches...etc.?
- Do you know of anyone who would want to harm you physically or mentally?

You can ask any question you feel is pertinent to aiding your investigation, just remember to be professional when doing so. These questions are not to pry, they are to help you in your investigation and to ensure that your team is safe and well-educated on the client.

Once you are satisfied with the validity of the claim and that you feel safe with the potential client, it is time to accept the invite to investigate their claims.

Remember, first and foremost, our job as a paranormal investigator is to help the client, regardless of whether you uncover proof of a haunting or not. You are a knight whose job it is to save those who cannot help or defend themselves from the paranormal or any other aspect of neglect, violence, or abuse.

Conducting the Investigation

The day has arrived. You and your team are ready to investigate your client's claim of paranormal activity. Make sure you arrive early, during the daylight hours. You will appreciate the sunlight when setting up your equipment.

Upon arrival to the site, the team will wait by their cars until the team leaders and one or two members of the team (leader's choice) meet with the clients to get a tour of the facility.

Now, the rest of the team will begin to move equipment into the building and begin setting up the command center.

Set Up the Command Center
Your tech manager should start setting up any stationary/security cameras at this point as well as any other equipment that needs to be established such as the command center. A command center should be a location either outside of the main structure being investigated or in a room that is far enough away from the main investigation area so as to not interfere with the investigation process. During the investigation, teams should stop by the command center to unwind, relax, grab some water, and review any anomalies they may have caught while investigating.

Meet with Home/Building Owner
Whoever oversees the investigation should meet with the owner of the structure, give them a rundown of what will transpire during the evening and take a tour of the more active areas. You may want to consider having the team sign a waiver that releases the client of all responsibility for any injury or illness the team may encounter during the investigation. Consider having a legal representative draft up an official release for use with your team.

The team leader should also get recorded statements from the home/business owner. A team lead should not share all of what they learned from their interactions with the client. You want your team to experience things organically, without the team leader's input influencing their investigation.

Establish Baselines
The investigative should make their way through the location and establish baseline readings for EMF and temperature and should take pictures and video of the structure while well-lit to thoroughly document the layout of the structure and each room within.

Lights Out
Now that equipment has been set up, the client briefed, and baselines done, the investigation can finally get underway. Depending upon your religious beliefs, it is suggested that the team gather together in the command center and bow their heads in prayer. They will speak a prayer of protection simply asking God to guide them and protect them and surround them in the white light of protection.

"Lights Out" simply means that you turn off the lights and begin your investigation.

People always ask why we go lights out, and the simplest answer I can provide is that it is just more fun. There is a certain creepiness factor that comes with walking around an allegedly haunted building in the dark. More times than not it is the only scary part of the investigation. But, there are some actual investigatory benefits to doing our work in the dark.

Our senses are heightened in the dark, we are more aware of our surroundings and we rely on our other senses to navigate. It should not be pitch black, mind you. You should have flashlights and nightlights to guide your path to a safe exit should you need to get out quickly. But we listen better when our vision is compromised. In the dark we may better hear audible evidence of paranormal activity.

The dark also eliminates any shadows cast from lamps or overhead lights, lessening the possibility of false positives in video and photographic evidence.

Investigate
Above all else, what you see on TV ghost hunting shows pertaining to an investigation is an often-truncated version of actual events. Investigations can take hours at the least, and days or weeks at the most to gather the evidence needed to substantiate a claim. Be willing to investigate the site as many times as is needed to feel content with your investigation.

For small locations requiring a small team of investigators (2 to 5-member team) your best bet is to stick together to avoid any accidental scene contamination.

For larger locations, you can send in several smaller teams, especially if there are multiple floors to cover. Each team should have a leader who is equipped with a 2-way radio that they will use to communicate with each other and with the command center.

As you walk through the house/business/structure, invite spirits to come forward.

Make sure that you are tagging any naturally occurring phenomenon (dogs barking, cars, passing, other investigators, etc.) caught on video and audio so that you don't falsely attribute it as paranormal activity in review.

As you go from room to room during the investigation, announce yourself and introduce yourself and the team to any spirits that might be present. Invite the spirits to come forward. Be sure to let them know that you mean no harm and that your equipment is intended to document their existence, not to harm them.

As you use your investigative equipment, explain out loud what you are doing so that you don't run off any spirits who may be unfamiliar with this modern technology.

During the investigation, you should be taking plenty of pictures, video, and conducting EVP sessions as previously described in this book. Keep your EVP and video sessions relatively short, as you will appreciate it when it comes time to review evidence.

Enter each room of the house/building. Respect the owner's wishes for you to avoid certain areas. Take plenty of pictures/video, ensuring only one person is taking photographs at a time. You don't want someone's flash or IR (Infrared/Nightshot) source contaminating your photos/video footage.

In each room take and document temperature readings several times to determine if there is any deviation from the established baseline.

In each room, take and document EMF readings to determine any deviation from the established baseline.

Pay close attention to your instinct. If your gut tells you to take a picture of a certain area, follow that instinct.

In each room, conduct ten-minute EVP sessions. (See the section on conducting EVP sessions earlier in this book).

You can conduct more than one session, but keep them at ten minutes or shorter, you will be thankful when it comes time to review these recordings later.

Do not provoke the spirits into showing themselves. It is disrespectful and dangerous. There may be times when provocation is necessary, but this will be determined by the team leader and carried out by someone with the knowledge of how to safely provoke spirits into responding.

Place trigger objects within rooms. For example, if the ghost is thought to be that of a child, place balls around the room and let the spirit know they can move the balls if they want. Or place toy trucks/cars on the floor and invite the ghosts to move those items.

During investigations, as you enter a room, be sure to announce yourself and speak in normal non-whispered tones. This is for the benefit of any member of your team who may have set up video or audio hardware to record the room. You do not want your whispering or unannounced presence in the room to be misidentified as paranormal activity.

Introduce yourself to the spirits. As you walk from room to room, let them know your name and where you are from. Allow them to feel comfortable with you. The more they sense that you are not a threat, the more forthcoming they will be with letting their presence known.

Encountering Paranormal Activity
Unlike television shows like Ghost Hunters and Paranormal State, you could go on a handful of investigations before you encounter anything remotely paranormal. This is a field of study that requires a lot of patience.

However, you will eventually encounter something that you simply can't explain and it will be a terrifying moment. Whether you see a shadow figure, a full-bodied apparition, see an inanimate object move by itself, or encounter any unexplainable phenomenon, the first thing you need to do is remain calm.

You have a built-in fight or flight mechanism that you will have to tuck away when encountering ghostly encounters. Don't run or scream. You are the professional and you have a client who expects a high degree of professionalism from the team he/she has allowed into their home or business.

If you have a video camera or a standard camera readily available, do your best to document what you are encountering. If you do not have the ability to capture photographic or video evidence, attempt to describe what you are seeing into your digital voice recorder. Be sure to include the date and time of the encounter as well as the exact location. Be as specific as possible. If you do not have a digital voice recorder, document what you can with your notepad and pen/pencil.

Ask others if then encountered any activity and compare notes. Do not share exactly what you saw as doing so could influence them to change their encounters to match yours. Everything needs to be documented and corroborated to act as proof, otherwise it is simply a personal encounter claim that can't be substantiated.

The types of paranormal activity you may encounter on an investigation include but are not limited to (and in no particular order):

- Knocking/scratching sounds
- Cold/warm spots
- Disembodied voices/vocal sounds
- Seeing shadow figures
- Seeing full bodied apparitions
- The sensation of being touched
- Hearing voices whispered in your ear
- The sensation of being watched/followed
- Seeing objects moved/manipulated on their own
- Feeling disoriented/nauseous
- Battery drain/power failure
- Power surges/lights going super bright then blowing out
- Interaction with a spirit (The spirit responds to your commands such as "knock once for yes, twice for no"
- Disembodied footsteps, the sound of someone walking around the room
- In rare instances, you may incur scratches or bites or be shoved/pulled

Take Breaks
Depending upon the size of the structure you are investigating, your time spent on an investigation can range from two and three hours for smaller venues, or sundown to sunup for larger venues. You will get exhausted during an investigation, so breaks should be a planned part of your night.

Everyone should return to the command center at several pre-planned intervals for a little rest and relaxation. Get off your feet, stretch out, unwind, and re-hydrate. Make sure you are getting plenty of fluids and that you have healthy snacks available. Avoid sugary snacks or energy drinks. You don't want to crash during an investigation. Keep fresh fruits, nuts, or meat snacks like beef jerky on hand to get an energy boost from proteins.

During breaks, be sure to check in with the team leaders and give them status updates, let them know what, if anything, you have encountered.

Use break time to replace batteries in flashlights and other battery powered equipment.

Talk with your fellow investigators, let them know of any areas of activity you have encountered so that they can check it out on their turn in that area of the house/building.

Closing Out the Investigation
You have just spent several hours walking around in the dark, conducting a thorough investigation. You may have encountered some paranormal activity, or, it may have been relatively quiet.

At the determined end of the investigation, the teams should leave the floor and return to the command center.

Pack up your personal belongings including any trash. You want to leave the scene in the same condition you found it. Respect your client's property as if it were your own.

If you borrowed any equipment from the team lead or any teammate, return it.

If you loaned any equipment, get it back.

The team lead may want to collect copies of your digital evidence (photos, videos, audio). If this is the case, do not leave without providing them these files.

Take the time to recap your experiences with your team, speak with each other about what you encountered to rule out any possible unintended/accidental contamination from your teammates. Do not start reviewing your evidence.

The tech manager will break down the command center with the help of anyone who has been designated to do so. They will break down cameras or any other equipment they have placed throughout the investigated environment.

If the homeowner/business owner is present, the team leader or director of investigations will meet with them, conduct a walkthrough to ensure everything is in good condition.

Set the appropriate turnaround for evidence review with the client. Do not tell them you will have an answer tomorrow if it will take a few days or more to review the hours and hours of evidence collected during the investigation.

Before leaving the grounds, the team should gather in prayer and ask God for protection and ensure that no spirits are bound to any member of the team. This will ensure any spirits that were present remain within the home and do not follow the investigator's home.

Everyone leaves together. No team members should be left at the building (inside or out).

CHAPTER 11: REVIEW YOUR EVIDENCE AND FINDINGS

If there is one thing that most television shows about the world of paranormal investigations tend to gloss over, it is the laborious process of evidence review.

I am here to tell you in no uncertain terms, that this portion of the process is often the worst. Conversely, it is also the most important as it will ultimately yield evidentiary support for the claims of a haunting.

Every group conducts evidence review differently. Some leave it up to the individual investigators to review their own evidence and report back to the team leader/director. Other groups have a team who are responsible for the review and logging of evidence.

It will be up to you as to how evidence gets reviewed and chronicled. It is about what works best for your group. Personally, I am a fan of the team who conducted the investigation reviewing their own evidence, as they were there and can best answer to the findings.

For evidence review, it might help to have everyone on the team focus on reviewing certain media. For example, one or two members of the team review all EVP evidence collected, another team member or two should focus on video, while others focus on photos, etc..

This method helps speed up evidence review as people are not having to switch between different programs and loading different types of media and changing focus.

If you are not conducting evidence review at a central

location and you are having your team review evidence from home, create an online drive through Google or Dropbox, or some type of online receptacle where discovered evidence can be dropped.

All positive evidence must be agreed upon by the group to include it as evidentiary support of a haunting in the final report to the client.

Reviewing EVP Evidence
- Use a set of high-end earphones that cancel out external noise. Ear buds are not recommended for evidence review
- Download an audio editing software tool such as Audacity
- DO NOT EDIT RAW FILES, if you need to raise the volume or add any filters to EVP files, save a copy and edit the copy. Protect the integrity of the raw files.
- Listen to each recording carefully, specifically during the moments of silence between each question
- Listen for voices that do not match the frequency/tone/voice of the investigative team. Remember, team members will not have been whispering.
- Listen for fade-ins and fade-outs, as if voices/noises are coming from and returning to a faraway place
- If you hear an anomaly, document the name of the recording and the time within the recording where the anomaly occurs.
- If you can determine what is being said, document it, but do not share with others what you believe is being said. Stop what you are doing and ask a fellow reviewer to listen to the recording. Ask them

what they think is being said and them write it down. Compare what you believe was said to what your fellow reviewer believes was said. If it is close or a match, you have a Class A EVP.
- Refrain from excessive editing of files. Manipulating even the most mundane sound too much can cause a false positive, transforming it into an EVP where there truly is none.

Reviewing Photographic Evidence
- If you are going to edit (lighten, darken, zoom in, zoom out, sharpen, etc...) a photo, make a copy first then edit the copy. Do not make changes to the originals.
- Review each photo carefully, starting by looking at the picture entirely, then going line by line through the picture.
- Do not zoom in too far, doing so distorts the image and can lead to false positives
- If you spot an anomaly, compare it to other pictures of the room including looking at the baseline photos to see if you can rule out a naturally occurring phenomenon
- You can choose to believe in orbs as proof of the paranormal if you wish, we do not. There are way too many things that can lead to the presence of orbs in photographs such as dust, bugs, and moisture. To us, orbs simply do not serve as proof of the paranormal.
- Be mindful of reflective surfaces such as windows and mirrors. A lot of false positives come about from reflections in these types of surfaces. But do not discount them as reflections so quickly. Study the image in the mirror. Does it appear to be contemporary or are there clothes or features that seem anachronistic (outside of the current time

period)? Does it seem humanoid or otherworldly? Can anyone on the team account for the reflection?
- Be educated on what can cause strange images in pictures. A streak or blur across a photo can often stem from someone lowering their camera before the picture is fully captured. This creates an unusual blur on a picture that is often confused with the presence of something paranormal.
- Look closely at the background of the pictures, in the dark recesses. If need be, lighten a copy the photo using photo editing software.
- If you suspect you have discovered evidence, write down what you believe you are seeing. Share the with the team but do not tell them what to look for. See if they can find the anomaly, then have them write down what they feel they are looking at. Compare your findings to theirs. If it is a match you have solid evidence. Otherwise, you might have some artifacting.
- Be mindful of pareidolia. This is a phenomenon where the brain attempts to make sense out of chaos in an image, such as making random blur or designs look like faces where there really isn't a face present. Our brains are wired to recognize faces, so when we are looking at a clutter of bushes, or condensation on a window pane, our brain attempts to fashion these random occurrences into a face. Be mindful that what looks like a face in a photo may be the result of pareidolia.

Reviewing Video Evidence
- As with audio evidence, video should have been recorded in small chunks to prevent the reviewer from having to sit through long video sessions.

- When reviewing video, keep an eye out for unnatural movements or for shapes that move in areas where nobody is present.
- Remember that shadows are not necessarily ghosts. Passersby cast shadows even in low light, especially if they are backlit.
- In addition to looking for visual proof of the paranormal, you should also be listening for audio evidence that may have been picked up by the camera's microphone. This can sometimes be used to corroborate EVP evidence as well.
- Do not edit any raw files. If you want to zoom in, zoom out, crop, or make any changes to the video to isolate incidents of paranormal activity, make a copy of the footage then make your edits to the copy. Maintain integrity of the raw file.
- If reviewing stationary camera footage, in addition to keeping an eye out for apparitions or figures, keep an eye on background objects such as lamps, curtains, or any trigger objects left in the room. These objects may be moved slowly over the course of the recording. It might not be noticeable without marking on the screen (or on the footage) the location of the object.
- Notate the name of the file and the minutes and seconds where any alleged activity occurs.
- If you capture video evidence of a haunting, write down what you see then share the video with a fellow reviewer. Have them review the evidence and write down what they believe they see. If your written assumptions match then you have video evidence of paranormal activity.

No matter what type of evidence you are reviewing, the goal is to find something to substantiate the claims of a haunting. You may have collected tens of hours of evidence and reviewed it thoroughly and not found a thing. This is perfectly fine. It simply means that during your investigation, there was no paranormal activity displayed to substantiate the claims.

What does that mean really? Does it mean the place is not haunted and the home/business owner lied?

Not at all. The client reached out to you as a last resort, it is a very real experience for them. They have most likely been encountering something they could not explain and need your help as the professional to identify just what is going on.

Ghosts and other supernatural entities are not circus animals. They do not perform on command and sometimes they will remain inactive in the presence of people with whom they are unfamiliar. Just because you couldn't prove a haunting doesn't mean there isn't something happening there.

Drafting a Final Report
Some paranormal investigation agencies choose not to write up a report of the investigation. Failure to do so is a disservice to both your agency and the clients you serve.

The length and thoroughness of the report will ultimately be up to you, but it should contain at the very least the following information:

- Date, start and end time
- Location of the investigation
- Names of members of the investigation team
- Weather conditions
- Moon phase

- Description of claims
- Breakdown of the investigation process (What was done, what rooms were investigated, personal experiences of investigators
- Evidence collection methods (Still photo, camcorder, digital voice recorder, dowsing rods, full spectrum, etc…)
- Breakdown of evidence collected (Total photos, hours of video recording, hours of audio recording, etc…)
- List of positive evidence (include the hh:mm:ss where evidence occurs in video and audio evidence)

Presenting Evidence to Your Client
With your investigation complete and your evidence reviewed, it is time to meet with your client and go over any evidence you may have found. Even if you didn't find any, you should still contact your client and meet with them in person to review what happened during the investigation and answer any questions they may have or provide them any helpful advice relevant to their situation.

If you have evidence to prevent, sit down with them at a computer if possible so that you can present your findings to them in real time. Review positive evidence with them, let them know what to look and listen for, and ask them if this is the type of experiences that have encountered.

Let the client review each piece of evidence. Be ready to answer questions they may have.

Here are some basic rules when reviewing evidence with the client:

1) Don't make it scary. Speak to them in regular tones, make them feel like this is ordinary. They are already

scared and unsure, there is no need to exacerbate the fear and uncertainty with theatrics.

2) Allow the client a few minutes to figure out what they are seeing/hearing and let them tell you what they think you have captured. If they are not seeing or hearing what you believe you have captured, then you can steer them in the right direction.

3) Share your personal investigation experiences, but set the expectation that these stories are not evidence as they do not support the claims with verifiable evidence. Stories are great to have, but they are not evidence and clients should be aware of this.

4) Allow the client to look at or listen to the evidence for as long as they want. Sometimes it takes a while to comprehend what they are experiencing. Do not rush them, allow them to fully soak in what has been captured. For many, it will be a relief as we are able to once and for all validate what they have been experiencing.

5) Be ready to provide comfort. Evidence reviews can be emotionally charged experiences. Clients could express fear, sorrow, confusion, and a myriad of other emotions that will require you to support. Don't be afraid to console your client.

6) Provide a lifelong line of communication to your client. You have already invested so much time and energy into the investigation. Just because the "fun" part is over, that doesn't mean you can forget the client. Let them know that you will be available for as long as they need you. Be ready to answer ongoing questions via email, phone, or in person visits.

7) Lastly, make sure they have a copy of all the evidence presented to them.

CHAPTER 12: CONCLUSION, OFFER BLESSING, & CLEANSING

With the investigation done and the evidence presented and the client satisfied with your outstanding work and care on their case, you are ready to move on to the next investigation.

Before you do though, consider offering your client one last piece of mind. You don't want to drop the bomb on them that they might very well have a presence in their home then wish them well as you drive off into the sunset.

As an investigative agency, it is your job to provide education, solutions, and if the client is so inclined, cleansings.

"Solutions" run the gamut of many things, ranging from links to paranormal information on the web, hooking the client up with local support groups, or providing tools and resources to the client for them to bring peace to their home.

One such service your group might choose to offer is a cleansing ritual, or blessing of the house.

Blessings and cleansings should be done by spiritual members of the group. Atheists and agnostics make darn fine investigators, but having them pray and bless the home would be like having a butcher cater a vegan wedding.

There are many resources you can check to figure out the best way to conduct cleansings and blessings. You will have to find the one that works best for you. Here is how Kindred Moon paranormal typically conducts a cleansing:

- Start with a basic prayer of protection. See the prayers and scriptures section of this book for basic protective prayers and spells you can say.
- Be sure you specifically identify that you are targeting negative spirits and energies, asking them to leave. Invite angels and positive spirits to stay if the client wishes.
- Place four Saint Michael the Archangel medals at the four corners of the property.
- Open a window or a door and begin in the furthest room from this open portal to the outside.
- Burn a white sage bundle as you walk slowly through each room of the house. (Open cabinets, closets and crawlspaces and allow the cleansing smoke to permeate these nooks and crannies.)
- Have the homeowner/client assert, "This is our home and you are not welcome here, you must leave this place." Command negative energy and spirits to leave the house.
- Members of the team should be saying prayers continuously as they walk from room to room.
- Slowly make your way with the burning sage to the open exit, driving the dark energy and spirits outside. Close the door or window, sealing out the energy once and for all.
- Make a sign of the cross in holy water on all the doors and windows leading into the home. to fully seal these entry points. Some investigators line thresholds with salt to prevent spirits and energies from crossing back into the house.

Once a house has been cleansed, it is imperative that the presence, or any other dark entity, not be invited back inside. The family must not allow fear, doubt, or anger permeate the home as these negative feelings are what draws unwanted spirits and demonic presences. Keep in mind, these spirits feed on these types of feelings.

The family should not willingly or knowingly invite spirits back into the house using Ouija boards or other sources of divination.

If small children are present in the home, they must be watched closely to ensure they do not talk to or welcome unseen visitors into the home.

A cleansing is only as strong as the family's willingness to maintain the sanctified stronghold put in place for their protection from these negative interlopers.

ADDENDUM: SHADOW BEINGS

Sooner or later, anyone who engages in paranormal investigations or has read about ghost/spirit hauntings, will encounter the topic of shadows and shadow beings.

While the study of shadows and shadow beings (aka shadow entities) is a whole field unto itself, as paranormal investigators we feel it is important to discuss the subject to some extent.

Shadow Beings, as the name suggests, are simply a dark black shadow figure. Sometimes the figure is wispy, other times more solid. The shape is usually humanoid, though non-humanoid (possibly animal) shapes have sometimes been reported.

The shadow's height typically ranges from three to seven feet tall. Sometimes faint facial features can be seen, most notably eye openings. On rare occasions, a full face is seen. The shadow usually doesn't show any signs of appendages.

Shadows seem to have the ability to move at a great speed. They can be seen standing still then quickly accelerate out of view. They do not seem to be contained by walls or other solid structures as they have been seen passing through them.

Shadows can be seen in both bright daylight or at night. Most often they are captured by photographic equipment (still photos or video) but have been seen with the naked eye. When seen with the naked eye they are often seen indirectly. That is, it's rare to look straight on at a shadow. Rather, they are seen peripherally. Some individuals seem more prone to viewing shadows than others. For these reasons, the very existence of Shadow Beings are subject to much criticism.

People often associated a sinister meaning to shadows, owing to the black color. This most likely is a false assumption. Black simply means the absence of emitted or reflected color. Whatever shadows are composed of, it's possible they do not emit or reflect any visible light (visible to the naked human eye at least) so they appear black to the human eye.

As previously mentioned the true nature of what shadows are is the subject of an entire field of study within the paranormal "industry" and is beyond the scope of this discussion. However, there are a few theories that should be reviewed:

- Ghosts/Spirit Manifestations – Some theorize shadows are just another way ghosts and spirits can manifest themselves. While not as common as the more usual white or bright light manifestation, it is possible that for whatever reason some spirits manifest more darkly. As mentioned before, whether this can be interpreted as having purpose or meaning is uncertain at best.

- Non-Human/Inhuman Entities – It is theorized that shadows are another class of paranormal entity, possibly representing non-human or inhuman entities. If so, whether they are angelic or demonic is not known.

- Aliens – Some believe that shadows are an alien life form. They could be the actual alien itself or a telepathic manifestation of their projection to our world. This theory isn't widely discussed or accepted as it leans so much towards science-fiction. But it deserves to be mention in the interests of completeness.

- 2-Dimensional Entities – Some have theorized that shadows are only 2 dimensional in structure (they have length and wide but no depth). It is theorized that shadows can only be seen when looked at by right-angles (i.e. 90 degrees or close to its profile). When viewed straight on or directly from behind they cannot be seen because they have no depth (thickness). When a shadow seems to appear, and disappear, it might just be turning from side profile to head-on and visa-versa.

- Alternate Life Forms – The sometimes-observed animal-like form of a shadow leads some to believe these are a type of rare and undocumented life form. Some paranormal researchers have taken video they believe shows a shadow in a very animal-like form. One video we have seen claims to show a shadow moving along the ground then "sprouting" wings and flying off. Since we did not take this video nor have access to the source LIPI is unable to perform an analysis of the claim.

There is no report we are aware of to indicate shadows are dangerous or threatening (other than their appearance). Some people have reported shadows moving small objects but there are other types of paranormal activity as well as non-paranormal events could also explain it.

To summarize, shadows and Shadow Beings (shadow entities) are an aspect of paranormal investigations. The probability of encountering a shadow is low compared to the other paranormal events that are more commonly reported. Still, investigators should be aware of the theories about shadows to better understand what they may encounter on an investigation.

Studies show that:

- Most shadow entities appear while a person is asleep, or about to fall asleep/wake up.
- They usually enter a room (or building) through a doorway but have been seen coming right through solid walls.
- Encounters can be occasional or throughout a person's lifetime. Sometimes they seem to "follow" a family from one generation to another.
- Encounters can start when people move to a new location. They sometimes are seen lurking in woods and undeveloped areas around buildings.
- The most commonly reported physical characteristics of a shadow are:
    - Tall 5-6 feet, sometimes 7 feet
    - Male in appearance
    - Dark and slim
    - Very black - "Blacker than black"
    - Looks like they are wearing a long black trench coat and a large brimmed hat
    - They appear to be 3-dimensional, opaque and seem to have physical mass
    - No eyes
    - Silent - they make no noise as they move but movement is clearly known
- They react when their presence is noticed, usually moving away very quickly
- They don't seem to obey common physical laws - can move through walls, unnaturally fast movement, can appear or vanish instantly.
- People often feel a sinister or mischievous feeling when they are encountered.

- Direct verbal communication is rare but some kind of thought-level communication sometimes appears to be occurring.
- Pets often react very negatively to them and places they have been
- They seem to "invade" your personal space
- She described 6 subcategories of shadows:
    - *Sentinels* - They stand in corners/edges and just watch us
    - *Lurkers* - They move through an area, often the same path over and over.
    - *Predators* - They seem to want to invoke intense fear/terror. Physical attack is sometimes reported.
    - *Visitors* - Groups of shadows. Often described as appearing otherworldly.
    - *MTB* - Minding Their own Business, similar to Lurkers they seem not to notice us as they move through an area.
    - *Omens* - Often appear just before a bad luck event or death happens. Often follow a person or entire family for generations.
    - *Haunters* - Are associated with accepted haunted locations
- Possible explanations for shadows include:
    - Ghosts/spirits
    - Shape Shifters
    - "Old Hag" legends
    - Thought Forms - beings that are formed out of our subconscious thought (like in the cinematic classic "Forbidden Planet" with Walter Pidgeon).
    - Ultraterrestrial beings - "Mothman"
    - Extraterrestrial beings - May be related to the M.I.B. (Men in Black) reports

- Things people can do to try to rid themselves of a shadow haunting:
    - Prayer
    - Spiritual cleansing
    - Mediate for emotional harmony
    - Change your environment
    - Sleep with the lights on (they rarely show during the day or in the light)

SUMMATION AND THANKS

The world of the paranormal is vast and varied. It is not an exact science and the field is littered with theories and possibilities. In the end, we are all in it together and serve one greater purpose:

To investigate and document positive proof of the existence of paranormal activity.

Fascination with the world of the supernatural is cyclical. It ebbs and flows. Interest wains for a period then suddenly peaks. It is your responsibility to use the downtime to educate yourself on new theories, investigate new entities (The Black Stick Man, Black Eyed Kids, etc…), and discover new equipment that will steer us closer to proving to the world that ghosts do exist and share this world with us.

You don't have to adhere to the Kindred Moon Paranormal way of doing things, obviously. You will find your own way in time. When you do, just ensure it is one of altruism, that you strive to serve your community, your peers, and the advancement of the field of paranormal research.

It is my sincere hope, that within this book you have found education, inspiration, and a jumping off point by which to start your own paranormal investigation team.

I want to thank you for purchasing this book. A lot of time and effort went into curating the information within and my gratitude for you taking the time to read it cannot be measured or easily put into words. If this book helps just one group find success, then my work here has been well worth the long nights, time away from friends and family, and countless hours of research and field work.

At the end of the day, we all have one goal, one unifying vision, and we all want the elusive proof that when we shuffle off our mortal coils, that we somehow go on. Proving the existence of ghosts and intelligent hauntings puts us one step closer to understanding what happens when our time has come to leave this world.

You have a world of fascination and wonder laid out before you. If you are just starting; embrace every aspect, learn as much as you can, and become the benchmark by which others in the field will be measured. This journey isn't just about you, it is about the elusive proof and the lengths we are willing to go to to find and document it.

I am glad that you are a part of it, my brothers and sisters. Thank you, and welcome to the family!

SPECIAL THANKS

Thank you to **Lorraine Warren**, the matriarch and queen of paranormal investigations with whom I have had the honor and distinction of working with, learning from, and forging a friendship with. Thank you for your support, wisdom, and love Lorraine.

A very special *thank you* to **Tony Harrington**, my dear friend, for whom without, this book would never have been finished. Thank you for all your help.

LINKS AND RESOURCES

About Kindred Moon Paranormal

Kindred Moon Paranormal is a group, assembled by founder Michael McDonald, whose purpose is to seek answers about the afterlife.

Michael has over thirty years of experience that he draws upon to propel this group of professionals in the field to be the best they can be.

Working free of charge, they set to rest the minds of families and business owners who experience unexplained occurrences.

Kindred Moon Paranormal Society continues the campaign to put ghosts into perspective and to empower people with paranormal wisdom.

Wielding state-of-the-art equipment and having vast knowledge of the supernatural, K.M.P.S. conducts their investigations logically and scientifically.

Kindred Moon Paranormal Society on the web

Official Website:

http://www.kindredmoonproductions.com/kmps.html

YouTube:

https://www.youtube.com/user/kindredmoon

Search Amazon.com for Kindred Moon Paranormal for a collection of original television programming featuring our investigations!

ABOUT THE AUTHOR

Michael McDonald is a paranormal investigator and founder of Kindred Moon Paranormal Society. He has over thirty years of experience in the world of paranormal research and investigation where he has worked alongside some of the field's most prominent names.

Michael resides in Missouri.

NOTES

Use these pages to document notable information from your own investigations, angel and demon names you have encountered, and any other information you deem pertinent or of high importance

_____
_____
_____
_____
_____
_____
_____
_____
_____

Made in the USA
Middletown, DE
17 July 2022